The Invitation

Mary LoVerde

WESTCOM PRESS

New York   Los Angeles   Washington DC

The Invitation
by Mary LoVerde

www.maryloverde.com

Published by: Westcom Press
                  2101 N Street, NW, Suite T-1
                  Washington, DC 20037

                  westcom.press@mac.com

ISBN - 978-0-9835003-8-4
ISBN - eBook: 978-0-9835003-9-1

Library of Congress Control Number: 2012908316

First Edition

Printed in the United States of America
18 17 16 15 14 13 12   4 5 6 7

I dedicate this book to my mother, Lou Schulte,
who has always supported my next steps.

Acknowledgements

I am blessed to have a circle of partners who believe in this book and me, and in the most generous ways helped me create it.

I want to thank the wise men and women who allowed me to share their stories. I have read their inspiring tales dozens of times and I am still in awe of their courage.

I wouldn't think of writing a book without my editor, Becky Cabaza. She is a genius with words and understands my voice and my mission.

My best friend, Brenda Abdilla worked off some serious karma after reading several versions of the manuscript and giving invaluable advice and encouragement.

I had many other readers as well. I offer special thanks to Kris Westphal, Donna Sorenson, Melanie Mills, LeAnn Thieman, Shelly Humbach, Karen Buxman, Sarah Hatfield, Emily Berchier, Nick LoVerde, Bill Schulte, Bruce Turkel, Lynn Price, Manisha Thakor, and Kym Miller.

This book was birthed in large part because of my collaboration with Sam Horn and Denise Brosseau, the two members of my mastermind group. Our three hearts and minds together create a rare and wonderful connection. I am eternally grateful to be in their midst.

A special nod goes to Chuck Canepa, who practices patiently with me, hour after hour, stretching and challenging me with the dance moves he knows but I am just learning.

I owe a debt of gratitude to Ann Luckett, Nancy Chen and Tina Menor who made it possible for Kauai to cradle me while I received the ideas for this book.

I thank my very first dance instructor, Jeanne Rifle Vaver. Your love of dance still lives in me a half a century later. And to my second dance instructor, my dad, Tom Schulte, who danced me around the living room while we watched The Lawrence Welk TV show.

My heart is full of gratitude for Artem Plakhotnyi, Inna Berlizyeva, Igor Ustymovych, (all three-time Ukrainian national champions) and Toni Therrien. I trained with these amazing instructors at the Imperial Ballroom studio in Scottsdale, Arizona, while I was in the final stages of completing this project. Their passion for dance and teaching re-lit a fire in me that was a powerful reminder why I want to help people take their next step.

And finally to the beautiful dancers everywhere who I strive to emulate and who inspire me to slip on my shoes and...step.

Table of Contents

Introduction

Dreaming of Lace and Sequins

We like to pretend it is hard to follow our heart's dreams. The truth is, it is difficult to avoid walking through the many doors that open. Turn aside your dream and it will come back to you again. Get willing to follow it again and a second mysterious door will swing open.

--Julia Cameron

One day I saw a bumper sticker that read, "What if the Hokey Pokey really IS what it's all about?" For those sophisticates who've repressed the memory of this dance song, it goes like this:

> *You put your right foot in.*
> *You put your right foot out.*
> *You put your right foot in and you shake it all about.*
> *You do the Hokey Pokey and you turn yourself around.*
> *That's what it's all about.*

1

This little ditty reminds me of the Disneyland song, "It's a Small World (after all)." Once you hear it, the melody and lyrics play in your mind incessantly, nearly requiring electroshock therapy to make it stop.

After I read that bumper sticker I had an interesting day of literally trying *not* to move my right foot in and out. I felt possessed. The darn thing tortured me until, upon retiring that night, a little voice said, "Maybe it's true. The Hokey Pokey *is* what it's all about."

Connection is what creates balance.

I have spent most of my adult life researching and presenting realistic ways to keep our busy lives in balance, writing books on the topic and globetrotting to speak to anyone who would sit still long enough to hear my message. I know for certain I am on the planet to do this mission, to help people understand that connection is what creates balance. Hearing the little voice, I was smart enough to recognize that the Universe, with Its creative sense of humor, had just planted a seed to help me live my mission more effectively--a seed, I would soon learn, that would take root and grow in unforeseen ways.

I did not always dream of lace and sequins. Growing up with five brothers I had ample opportunity to be a tomboy and play any kind of ball: base, basket, foot, soft, golf, stick, dodge; you name the ball, our family threw it, caught it, and hit it. I come from a long line of athletes and genetically have a natural ability that made my brothers and their friends tolerate my participation. I knew not to cry or I would end up kicked out of the game and inside the house ironing pillowcases. The boys knew not to make me cry because they needed me to even up the teams.

Then one glorious day, at age eight, my mother took me to my first dance lesson. I was very shy back then (unbelievable, say my friends now) and I can remember my reluctance walking into the basement of Riffle's Dance Studio. But as my lesson began my mother says I lit up like a Christmas tree. Something moved in me, and all I could think of was dance. I felt girly and beautiful and alive. Soon I was dancing at recitals, necessitating my master seamstress mother to stay up all night sewing the lace on my red and white polka dot maid costume (for our "Merry Maids" number, of course) or the ever-so-cute tail on the white bunny costume with pink sequins.

Forget my brothers. Forget the balls. *I was dancing.*

I was hardly a prodigy, but playing all those sports with my brothers ("Mary! Keep your arm straight...you throw like a girl! Watch your left foot! Now follow through! Faster! Too fast--slow it down!") taught me how to move and gave me a strong sense of where my body was in space. Dance is a performance art and I loved being in front of an audience. I remember one summer performing in a recital at the Des Moines County Fair. My dance team, Nancy, Lois, Merrilee and I were a preadolescent group of girls of widely disparate sizes. All dressed in our favorite polka dot costume we stood on the big stage, smiling out at our families and a crowd of what I remember as at least 1000. (It was probably ten people--you know how memories are.)

We were tapping up a routine that would make Sammy

Davis, Jr. proud when a little problem occurred. The record player sat on stage with us and each time we got to the vigorous "shuffle-ball-change" part of the routine, the needle would jump on the vinyl and skip ahead. We were so out of sync we must have looked like a bad "Saturday Night Live" skit. All I remember was how good it felt to be in those sequins and lace--and to dance.

On one of the few truly sad days of my childhood my beloved teacher, Jeannie Riffel, moved away from our quaint midwestern town of 900 people, and with no other dance instructor for miles and miles of cornfields, my dancing days came to an abrupt and disappointing halt. So, of course, I joined the girls' basketball team.

Fast-forward through a stint playing high school and college basketball, marriage, and labor and delivery. I still longed to dance, but with a full-time job, three children, a husband and a mother-in-law to take care of, my plate looked like I was always going through the all-you-can-eat buffet. My two daughters danced for a few years and when I dropped them off at their classes I often wanted to grab a cane and top hat and do an Ann Miller impersonation. (Google Ann Miller if you like. God, she had gams.)

When the kids were all old enough to tie their shoes by themselves I took dance lessons with my husband, who admitted that he had fantasies that he was the Father of Rhythm. He *was* the father of our three children, but not the Father of Rhythm. He lasted three sessions.

Life races by. One day I looked up, and saw that my 28-year marriage was over, my uterus was gone, and my bank account post-divorce had just under 11 dollars. My grown children were moving out, then in, then back out again, each time taking things they thought I wouldn't need anymore, like the kitchen table and the living room lamps.

I knew it was time to start again and create a new life for myself. I saw this unexpected turn of events as a clear invitation to let go, open up and reach out. I was being asked to grow and expand and I firmly believed I'd been called to an exciting world of new ideas and new ways of being and doing.

> I saw this unexpected turn of events as a clear invitation to let go, open up and reach out.

And while I like to think I can embrace a good ole fashioned transformational experience with the best of 'em, in truth, while I appreciated the invitation, I was really not at all thrilled about being on this particular guest list.

I hadn't the foggiest notion about how to move forward. Usually the eternal optimist, I now felt afraid, unsure and stuck. Bewildered. Angry. Beat. Mostly I felt lost. Yes, most definitely lost. I didn't know where to go or how to get there, and I couldn't answer perhaps the most important question I'd ever faced:

How do I take the next step in my life?

As luck would have it, the delicious force known as synchronicity took over.

Each January 1st I hold a "Goal Collage" party. The group of ten or more ladies, who are spiritually inclined and who love to drink wine all afternoon while scanning magazines for things that represent their fondest desires, show up at my house to glue these glossy representations onto poster board. I am sure you have seen how to make these vision boards on "Oprah." Over the years we have manifested some pretty amazing things from this project, enough to make you start believing in your mood ring again.

One New Year's day, while I was in the midst of struggling mightily with what my "next step" might be, my goal collage had no less than six pictures of various women in beautiful ball gowns. I had absolutely no conscious idea why.

Out of the blue one of my friends said she was taking dance lessons. Immediately lights flashed in my mind and I swear I could hear a host of angels singing Shakira's "Hips Don't Lie." I knew what I had to do. One phone call led to another and six days later the gowns on my collage made sense. My long ago retired dreams were about to come true.

I began taking ballroom dance lessons on January 7, 2008 at 2 pm.

Forty-six years after my last dance lesson, I again, less shy this time, walked into a studio where I met my new private ballroom instructor, a tall, dark, handsome, sexy, (happily married) Latino dance machine named Manny Viarrial. One step and I was addicted, and I immediately knew I had no plans for rehab.

The addiction grew. Shortly after my first lesson with Manny I also began taking lessons at Booth's DanceSport

Studio in Denver. My instructor there, Taylor Westfall, is a 26-year-old, classically trained, award-winning instructor and amazing performer who could easily play the handsome romantic lead in one of those vampire movies.

And I get to dance with both these men every week.

It is *so* good to be me.

I feel about my dance lessons now the same way I feel about my hysterectomy. Why did I wait so long?

Who knew that when I asked the question, *"How do I take the next step in my life?"* that the Universe, again with Its creative sense of humor, would literally answer me by teaching me *dance* steps. But that is exactly what happened. Each dance lesson turned into a profound and often hilarious life lesson. Not infrequently I had to stop in the middle of the session when a huge "aha" hit and I'd quickly scribble on a scrap of paper what the instructor said. The message was not subtle. Manny or Taylor may have been talking about dance but I clearly heard the real meaning intended for me. I gratefully received the answers to my question.

And now, this book is an invitation for you to take *your* next step.

Many times throughout our lives we ask that same question, "How do I take the next step?" There are the normal rites of passage when the question pops up, for example, when we graduate from high school or college, start job hunting, get married/partnered, decide whether/when to begin a family, buy a house, change careers, go back to school or retire. Sometimes the question is thrust upon us with a marriage or divorce, a birth, job loss or promotion, foreclosure, company merger, injury, health issues or the death of a loved one. Other times we simply ask the question of ourselves, knowing that we must move forward to live the life we have always dreamed of. Go big or go home.

We can easily recognize these pivotal invitations in our lives, but actually I have come to understand that every day begins with an invitation. Each morning when we open our eyes a life force surrounds us, fills us, and beckons us to accept the invitation to move forward. We are summarily summoned to a planetary party where we are the guests of honor. It is then our responsibility to RSVP with an enthusiastic *yes*.

Every day begins with an invitation.

In this book you will learn just as I did how to take the next step. Each chapter opens with a dance/life lesson and expands into concrete ideas that work in real life. Eventually you will get to a section called a *Case in Point*, featuring an inspiring person who used that particular lesson to take an extraordinary next step. The dancers out there will read the phrase as "en pointe," which is the extremely difficult ballet technique of dancing on the tips of your toes--the ideal metaphor for these real-world stories featuring remarkable women and men who are so out-of-this-world inspirational that you might stop reading and wonder, "For God's sakes, where did she find these people?" I did not have to look far. I am proud to say I found them right in my own life. They are my family, friends, and colleagues, most of whom I have known for decades, who beautifully illustrate the power of the human spirit. Throughout the book I will also share ideas from the many readers who write to me and enlighten me with their take on these issues.

At the end of each chapter you will find a section titled *Accepting the Invitation,* where I spotlight a special correspondence that I think brilliantly demonstrates why taking the next step is so very worthwhile. I'll recap the chapter in a section called *The Lesson,* which is followed by a vitally important question, under *Take Your Next Step.* I believe you will gain the most if reading this book is an interactive process, so I invite you at the end of each chapter to respond to this question, by writing how you will use the lesson to take *your* next step. You may also find these responses helpful if you choose to further explore how you can move forward at IAcceptThe Invitation.com.

Throughout this book you will find many spiritual references, so let me say this up front: You may celebrate Hanukkah, have a fish on your car bumper, or make a water offering at your temple. Perhaps you say the rosary, pray five times a day kneeling east, or smoke ganja to reach enlightenment. You might consider the golf course your church every Sunday morning or maybe you are more like my friend, Kris, who often quips to me, "See you in church-if you're sitting by the window." *It is none of my spiritual business what you believe or how you worship.* Please read and enjoy this book in your own way.

And now, you are invited to turn the page and begin.

Chapter One

Ask

As a single footstep will not make a path on the earth, so a single thought will not make a pathway in the mind. To make a deep physical path, we walk again and again. To make a deep mental path, we must think over and over the kind of thoughts we wish to dominate our lives.

--Henry David Thoreau

*S*o, are you ready to accept the invitation to take a step in a new direction? Good.

First, I'd like you to ask yourself, *"What do I really want?"* I mean, really *really* want.

You may sit down and journal the answer. Perhaps you will hit tennis balls or fold laundry or go out into your garden while you dig deep for the answer. Maybe you'll play Bubble Trouble on your iPhone or retreat to your man cave or Nordstrom's shoe department. You will know what to do and where to go to hear the clear honest answer.

It could take a while for the truth to reveal itself. The process of asking awakens you to the power you have to manifest the life you want. The answer creates a positive expectation, either consciously or unconsciously. As you think about what you want a desire pulses in you and that sets you up for the second part of the asking equation. Once you know what you want, then you ask the Universe to deliver it. You cannot skip this step. As prosperity teacher Edwena Gaines points out, the biblical phrase is, "Ask and you shall receive". It is not, "Make me guess."

So how does the asking technique work, you wonder? To explore the process of asking the Universe for what you desire let's go back to my goal collage. In addition to the six ball gowns on my vision board I had this picture:

Photo on my collage January 1, 2008

Again, as with the ball gowns, I did not consciously know why I chose this particular photo, but after years of doing this exercise I knew not to argue with my higher self. I cut the photo out of the magazine and glued it onto my board.

I completed the collage January 1. On February 24 I got a voice mail from a really great guy who I'd known and admired for 15 years. He left me the following message: "I'm on the way to the airport where I will meet up with a group of wonderful friends for a long weekend. I want you to join me. Meet me in the Dominican Republic... tonight."

My first reaction was, "What? Are you nuts?" Though I had quite a crush on him, I was reluctant to accept this invitation because, truth be told, for nine months I had been nursing a broken heart after a break up with my boyfriend, and I was pretty committed to the pity party I hosted each night. Was I really ready to take the next step? To dry my tears, get off the sofa and move on? His call prompted me to consider whether it was finally time for me to start living that part of my life again with zest. No, I wasn't nuts--I was ready. I decided that once in every woman's life she deserved to get a voicemail that says, "Meet me in the Dominican Republic... tonight," and once in every man's life he deserved to hear her say, "Yes." So throwing caution to the trade winds, I secured a ticket, packed my leopard print bikini and drove to the airport.

I woke up the next morning in the Caribbean, walked out the back door of my hotel room on the beach level and this is what I saw:

Photo outside my hotel room February 24, 2008

You can only imagine my reaction. And yet, on another level, although I was certainly impressed, I was not surprised in the least. I had words and photos all over my collage that showed I clearly knew what I wanted: romance, beauty, order, fun, exciting travel and adventure. Making the collage was my way of asking the Universe for it. As I said, my friends and I had been using this method for years to successfully manifest our hearts' desires.

Still, I wanted to know the science behind this. How exactly does it work that one day I am in my kitchen sipping wine, flipping through magazines and cutting out a picture of a perfect beach thousands of miles away and 55 days later I am *in* that photo?

I spent 15 years as a medical researcher so to answer the question I reverted back to my old habits and began conducting what scientists call a review of the literature. I discovered that no matter whom I consulted, from Rumi to Aristotle, from the Bible to Einstein, from Dear Abbey to Wayne Dwyer, they all said the same thing:

Everything in the universe starts with an intention.

They unanimously advised, therefore, if you want to take the next step in life, first set a clear intention of what you want. Who was I to argue with the all-time greats?

While this did not answer all my questions, it did point me in the right direction to continue my research. I was willing to accept the importance of an intention but first I had to know what that word meant. I went to the dictionary and to the intention guru, Dr. Deepak Chopra, author of *The Spontaneous Fulfillment of Desire*. Consider these definitions:

Intention--

- an anticipated outcome that guides your planned action
- a purposeful plan to perform an action that leads to a desired result
- a course of action that one intends to follow
- a force of nature; a thought you have that helps fulfill a need

Okay, I thought. *Setting* an intention seemed simple enough. But what about the next part? How do you go from setting an intention to getting what you want?

How Intentions Really Work

When I talk freely about intentions, the Universe, Source, God, and manifestations, my friend, Kris, squints her eyes, wrinkles her forehead and tilts her head to one side, like a cute cocker spaniel unclear about what she's been asked to do. Perhaps you, too, are thinking that surely there has to be something a little more sophisticated going on with intentions than simply gluing pictures on poster board. The answer is, well, yes and no.

During the course of my research I came across Lynne McTaggart's brilliant book, *The Intention Experiment.* In it she offers a fascinating array of scientific studies showing how intentions work. Many of these studies report findings so convincing they make the power of intentions nearly irrefutable.

To understand how intentions work let's start with a quick lesson in quantum physics, one of the scientific areas

McTaggart explores. The pioneers in this field discovered that the subatomic world actually follows rules that they had never seen before.

First, the scientists discovered the tiniest bits of the universe, the fundamental units that make up subatomic particles called **quarks**. (Only because I think it is interesting and funny let me add here that scientists have named the six "flavors" of quarks: up quark, down quark, top quark, bottom quark, charm quark and strange quark. Who says quantum physicists don't have a sense of humor?)

The scientists learned that quarks are not orderly little systems but something far messier: tiny clouds of probability. Quarks, much to everyone's amazement, are not stable and solid things, like atoms and molecules. Quarks exist only as a potential of what they can be in the future. I read that concept and thought, "Huh?"

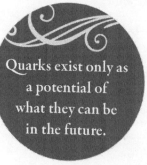

Quarks exist only as a potential of what they can be in the future.

And it gets weirder. McTaggart writes, "The only thing dissolving this little cloud of probability into something solid and measurable was the involvement of an observer. Once the scientists decided to take a closer look at a subatomic particle by taking a measurement, the subatomic entity that existed as pure potential would 'collapse' into one particular state."

McTaggert explains that these findings have huge implications regarding how intentions work:

1. "Living consciousness somehow is the influence that

turns the *possibility* of something into something *real.*"

2. "Not only does the observer bring the observed into being, but that nothing in the Universe exists as an actual thing before that."

3. "Reality is not fixed but fluid, and hence, possibly open to influence."

If your eyes have now rolled back into your head in confusion while reading all this physics stuff I am right there with you. I quoted McTaggert directly because I was not sure how to paraphrase the information without convoluting it. My brain is not capable of comprehending the minutest of all particles that do not really exist until I look at them. Dr. Chopra says not only are quarks stranger than you think they are, they are stranger than you can think. (I felt better when I heard that. It seems to me perhaps the flavors should all be called strange quark.)

For 30-plus years the most prestigious quantum physicists in the world have been studying whether thinking certain directed thoughts could affect one's own body, inanimate objects and virtually all manner of living things, from single-celled organisms to lab animals to other human beings. Some of these scientists have produced remarkable results showing that human intentions can affect the direction in which fish swim, the movement of gerbils, rats, cats, and dogs and the breakdown of yeast, algae and other cells in the laboratory. (They have not yet determined why men won't put the toilet seat down but they're working on it. The secret must lie in quantum physics. We've considered everything else.)

It's Not Just Homo Sapiens

The story gets even stranger. Animals themselves proved capable of acts of effective intention. McTaggert describes one ingenious study at the Fondation ODIER in Nantes, France, in which a robotic mother hen (which undoubtedly looked nothing like a real hen) "was imprinted on a group of baby chicks soon after birth. The robot was placed outside the chick's cage, where it moved around freely, as its path was tracked and recorded. Eventually it was clear that the robot was moving toward the chicks two and one half times more often than it would have ordinarily; the 'inferred intention' of the chicks--their desire to be close to their mother--appeared to affect the robot, drawing it closer to the cage."

Over eighty similar studies have reproduced this remarkable result!

When I read the mother hen/robot study I thought, "This all borders on being unbelievable, perhaps even suspect," so I think it's important to emphasize here that these results come from world-famous scientists conducting the most rigorous research. They are not a bunch of woo-woo, nut cases (not that I have anything against woo-woo or nut-cases, per se). These men and women have buildings and institutes named after them. Their professional reputations rely upon having complete confidence in their reported findings, including scientific results that have been reproduced by many other equally reputable academic researchers.

McTaggert made it easier to understand when she wrote, "Intention appears to be something akin to a tuning fork, causing the tuning fork of other things in the universe to resonate at the same frequency. It's not a special gift, but a learned skill, readily taught."

Everything that happens in the universe starts with an intention.

Let me say it again. The scientific bottom line appears to be this:

Everything that happens in the universe starts with an intention.

A New Way to Look at Things

Once you believe in intention, it's really fun to watch all the "coincidences" and opportunities that start showing up.

Sir Edmund Hilary, the first man to summit Mount Everest, is often quoted because of his astounding accomplishment. Beyond that, when you read his words below, consider that what he says is not only true, but that there are now mountains of scientific research that back up his reflections on the concept of intention:

"Until one is committed, there is hesitancy, the chance to draw back, always ineffectiveness. Concerning all acts of initiative (and creation), there is one elementary truth, the ignorance of which kills countless ideas and splendid plans: that the moment one definitely commits oneself, then Providence moves too.

All sorts of things occur to help one that would never otherwise have occurred. A whole stream of events issues from the decision, raising in one's favor all manner of unforeseen incidents and meetings and material assistance, which no man could have dreamed would come his way."

You might be thinking, "What does this have to do with

intention?" Knowing what the quantum physicists have discovered, Sir Hilary's quote might now go something like this:

"Until one has observed the quark, there exists only a potentiality, a mere cloud of probability, like unset Jell-O. Concerning all acts of initiative (and creation), there is one elementary truth, the ignorance of which kills countless ideas and splendid plans: that the moment one sets an intention, then Wave particle A and Wave particle B move, too.

All sorts of subatomic particles collapse, creating matter that would never otherwise have materialized. A whole stream of events issues from the intention, raising in one's favor that the quantum particles will develop an astonishing ability to influence one another and retain an eerie remote hold over each other without regard to time and space, creating synchronicities and miracles, which no man could have dreamed would come his way."

As my Italian neighbor Lucy likes to say, "Same, same."

There's More

Gregg Braden, an internationally renowned pioneer in bridging science and spirituality and the author of *The Spontaneous Healing of Belief* has a lot to say about the details of collapsing quarks.

"Research shows beyond any reasonable doubt that the (quantum) field responds to us--it rearranges itself--in the presence of *heart-felt feelings and beliefs*," he writes. In other words, when we say, "I believe it with all my heart" our heart's electrical and magnetic fields go nuts with activity, communicating with our brains and every cell within us.

Scientists have measured these fields eight feet beyond the body, and confide they probably extend for miles beyond where the heart physically resides. Studies by the Institute of HeartMath have shown that the heart's magnetic field is 5000 times stronger than that of the brain. When we set an intention and think of it in our brains and then also feel it in our hearts we create waves of energy that speak to the world "in every moment of every day through a language that has no words: the belief-waves of our hearts."

> There must be emotion underlying our intentions.

Bottom line: There must be emotion underlying our intentions. Without it, all we have is a vague wish and, based on a whole lot of hard-core research, a wish is not quite enough to make the pony appear.

In addition, Braden says research shows we also have to visualize the intention as if it has already been manifested. Collapsing the quarks into the matter we desire is less about *making* something happen and more about *believing it already has.* Yes, this concept goes against everything most of us have been taught. But remember, we are talking about waves and particles that can be in one place only, two places at once or even many places simultaneously. They can communicate with each other in the past, present and future. Braden says, "To a quantum particle then is now and here is there."

My point being these little darlings just get stranger and stranger but the research from around the world continues to confirm what is hard for us to wrap our gray matter around:

We really will see it when we believe it. And we believe it when we feel it.

Say that fast three times.

So let's review for a moment. To move forward we must

- Be crystal clear about what we want
- Set an intention
- Believe it and feel it with all our heart
- See it as completed and feel grateful.

No, there will not be a quiz later.

If at this point you have started to zone out and you've poured yourself a glass of wine and said aloud, "What the hell is she talking about?" all that means is you do not have a Ph.D. in quantum physics, which is what it would take for this to all make sense.

Why try to explain quarks in a book about taking the next step in life? The reason why I made a soft landing into some hard science is because I want to add depth to our understanding of the power of setting an intention. I am quite capable of having faith that seasons change and the sun comes up in the morning and sets in the afternoon, all in divine order. I also like to know that scientists have proven the earth orbits the sun and this planet I am riding on turns on its axis every 24 hours. I think faith and science are two parts of the whole and ignoring either of them keeps us from really understanding the big picture.

Case in Point: Island of Intention

Writing this book itself was an exercise in the concept that everything begins with an intention. I had written my first three books in Hawaii while I taught graduate classes there each summer. Blessedly the words flow to me easily on these sacred islands. So I set an intention to write this book in Kauai. Two years ago, I wrote the introduction on the north shore in Princeville, nearly verbatim to what you read here. The words felt dictated to me. A year passed and I returned to the same location and wrote what is now Chapter Two, on quitting. One chapter a year is an intention, but it's at a pace that makes one's literary agent age prematurely. I knew it was time to get serious.

During this particular trip to Princeville, I found myself sitting on the beach next to beautiful 39-year-old Nancy. A group of us were gathered around the bonfire, listening to her story of how she had recently fallen in love with a man in California. Nancy and I immediately felt an affinity for each other. We met again a few nights later at her condo for a glass of champagne and a wonderful evening of heartfelt, deeply insightful girl talk. I was flying home to Denver the next day and Nancy was moving to California in a couple of weeks. We wondered if we might be able to see each other on the mainland.

The next day my friend, Brenda, and I were sitting at the pool, having our last Mai Tai and mahi-mahi sandwich before heading to the airport. Tina, our delightful "local" server, asked rhetorically, "How are you?" With my lip in a pout, I said, "Actually, I'm so sad to leave the island. I am not ready to go home."

She smiled, "Well, you could come back and be my room-mate." We all laughed at the absurdity, and I thought, "I sure wish I could."

When Tina came back with the bill she said, "I'm not joking. I have two roommates who are not getting along and one of them will move out in three weeks. Here is the telephone number of my landlady. Come be my roommate."

I began to think this invitation through. Why couldn't I come back? I can do my work on a computer from anywhere, I reasoned. With the slow economy I did not have a speech scheduled in February. I was recently empty-nested and I had a trusted assistant in Denver to watch over my house in my absence.

I realized I was living my life as though I was penned in. Like a dog wearing a collar even after the electric fence had been turned off, I had not figured out that I could leave my back yard and go have an adventure.

Infinite possibilities were beckoning.

Before taking off to LAX I called Tina's landlady from the Lihue airport and left her a message. I got on the plane and turned to Brenda and said, "I'm coming back here for the month of February to write. I am not sure exactly how but I know I will."

A couple of days later I got a call from Tina explaining that her roommates had kissed and made up. She was sorry, but there was no room at the inn. Well, good for them, I thought. But the seed had been planted and my intention was clear. My heart was already in Kauai.

Immediately I wrote to my friends on the island and asked them to put the word out that I needed a bed and a place to make a simple meal for the next month. A few days later Nancy, my new beach friend, wrote that she was having second thoughts about permanently moving out of her condo before she knew things would work out in California. She wondered if I would like to house-sit at her condo for the next month. I would just have to cover her very reasonable rent and she would throw in the use of her car for free.

Would I!

I had been to her beautiful home and it was exactly where I wanted it to be on the island. I had enough frequent flier miles for a free ticket. And I had a book to finish.

On top of all that, without any pre-coordination on our part, I landed a few hours before she left, she picked me up, and we dined together. I took her back to the airport and drove off to the condo in her car. Those quarks were collapsing in perfect synchronicity.

Okay, It's Your Turn Now

Six pictures of ball gowns turn into dance lessons a week later. A photo of a thatched umbrella on a beach becomes a romantic vacation spot in less than two months. The perfect Hawaiian writer's retreat lands in my lap at just the right time. What is that all about? The power of intention is

Tell the Universe you are ready to receive.

getting harder for humankind to argue with. Unbelievable as it may seem, there is mounting, peer-reviewed, scientific evidence along with anecdotal reports galore, to prove that thoughts really *are* things and they *create* things out of nothingness. I think it is worth the risk to go along with the idea.

To take your next step, you must first ask yourself, "What do I want?" Do not move quickly through this step. It is the foundation of everything else that will follow. Then, set your intention—and **let it happen.** You can set your intention using a tool like the collage as I did or in the form of a written or spoken statement. *Tell the Universe you are ready to receive.* The quarks will be all over your project. You do not have to know *how* it will happen nor are you in charge of *making* it happen. Dr. Chopra says you just have to allow it to happen. "The less we interfere with it," writes Chopra, "the more we see that it has its own infinite organizing power."

Accepting the Invitation

Dear Readers,

While science is still working out the innumerable details of the best ways to collapse particles into your desired material and spiritual reality, scientific data support a few how-to's regarding setting your intention.

Find a quiet place that feels good to you.

1. *Still your mind in meditation.*
2. *State your intention in the present tense as a fact that has already been achieved. Be specific about your intention. Then add, "I intend for this or something better for the highest good of all."*
3. *Visualize in your mind's eye the desired result. Imagine yourself in the situation as if it already exists.*
4. *Feel your emotions. Get your heart involved.*
5. *Believe in the power of intention and in what you have intended.*
6. *Express your gratitude.*
7. *Release your intention into the Universe.*

Good luck!
Warmly,
Mary

THE LESSON: *ASK*

Ask yourself what you really want.
Set your intention.
See it.
Feel it.
Believe it.
Allow it to happen.
Say thanks.

Take Your Next Step

What is it that you really want?

Chapter Two

Quit

"Never quit." What a spectacularly bad piece of advice. It ranks right up there with "Oh, that's a funny dirty joke, let's tell the teacher."

--Seth Godin

I arrived at my first dance lesson in nearly half a century feeling like I was at Yankee Stadium, throwing out the first pitch of the season. I knew I wasn't a major leaguer but I did want to at least get it across the plate. Manny, my new instructor, greeted me in his trademark warm way, then started the music and took me for a little test drive to assess my dancing abilities. Most students have danced before and chances are they have some bad habits. I was no exception. It became immediately apparent that I flap my arms. Think back to your high school dances. I'm sure I am not the only one who pumped her arms up and down to find the beat. Flapping made sense to me. It felt comfortable and I was certain I looked quite sexy doing it.

Ever the professional (and holding back what had to be a knee-slapping belly laugh) Manny matter-of-factly announced, "There is a 'no flapping' provision somewhere in my contract." Apparently the Funky Chicken is not a sanctioned ballroom dance.

As the lesson wore on, the list of little tics I needed to eliminate grew. I leaned on him, did a weird little flick with my right foot, rolled my shoulders forward and persistently tilted my head to the side. I also ducked when I did an under-arm turn. Just like there is no crying in baseball, there is, I came to learn, no ducking in dance. Worst of all my bad habits, I regularly looked down to see what my feet were doing. Manny would smile and ask, "Checking for cockroaches?"

"First," he instructed me, "you must quit the movements that do not contribute to the dance. Then, I'll teach you what to do instead." Despite my skepticism he insisted it was indeed possible to quit flapping and still stay on the beat.

My first lesson reminded me of the often-told story about Michelangelo after he had sculpted his famous masterpiece, David, from a block of stone. When asked how he could carve so exquisitely the artist answered that he just removed everything that was not David.

I had to remove everything that was not the dance.

Driving home from the studio I thought about the concept of quitting and remembered the adage I'd grown up with:

A quitter never wins.
A winner never quits.

That old saw made some sense back when I was playing basketball with my brothers, the score was tied, and we had two minutes on the clock to win the game. It made sense on some really bad days at work, when I sucked it up and stuck it out and was rewarded with a really brilliant result. But now, at this stage in my life, I'd come to realize that much of what I'd been told about being successful had been inaccurate, especially the so-called truisms that include "always" and "never." Experience—from job loss to failed relationships--had taught me that in some cases the truth turned out to be exactly the opposite of what I'd long believed.

So I decided to become a quitter. I quit flapping, flicking, leaning, rolling and tilting. After several lessons I even quit ducking. I immediately became a better dancer. Getting rid of those liabilities prepared the way for me to learn my new steps. Quitting, it seemed, was making me a winner.

A Broader Application: The Argument for Quitting

I was quite intrigued with my lesson on quitting. Eager to learn what others thought about the concept I wrote an essay about it for my Internet readership:

Winners Quit

Quit abusive relationships. No one deserves this.
Quit smoking. It's stupid to put carcinogens in your lungs in the name of pleasure.

Knowing what to quit, when to quit, how to quit and why you are quitting is the hallmark of an authentic life.

Quit complaining if you're not going to back up your bitching with action. *You are powerful. Act.*

Quit saving the good champagne for a special occasion. *If you are strong enough to pop the cork, that's special enough. Celebrate life.*

Quit holding a grudge. *Forgiveness will set you free.*

Quit telling negative stories in your head. *Tell a new story the way you want life to be and watch what happens.*

Quit thinking you're not good enough. *Thinking it only makes it so.*

Quit looking for a pill to make you happy and healthy. *Eat fruits and vegetables, sleep for eight hours a night, exercise regularly, meditate, and connect with your family, friends and faith. Love life.*

Quit jobs you hate.

Yes, even in tough markets. You won't succeed there, anyway.

Quit beating yourself up. *You are lovable.*

The real truth is **winners quit.**

Knowing what to quit, when to quit, how to quit and why you are quitting is the hallmark of an authentic life.

So by all means, please, please quit.

My Internet readers responded in droves when I asked for their response to my question, "What are you willing to quit?" They passionately fired right back with the flapping and ducking that they committed to stop doing. My readers seemed grateful for the reminder that releasing what is not working creates space for new ideas and innovative solutions, which can powerfully propel us forward.

What to Quit

My yoga instructor Eagle (yes, that's really his name) has a consistent answer to nearly every question I pose. "Inquire within," he'll advise me. So if you are wondering what should be on your elimination list, get quiet and ask yourself the question, "What do I need to quit to take the next step?"

Many of the answers will come quickly because you already know a lot of what's in the way. You've probably tried to get rid of the barriers before. So acknowledge them. Ask them to sit down with you and say your goodbyes. Some of them have been like family to you. There is a part of you that will miss them, but like a jealous lover who hangs on too tightly, you know deep down you'll both ultimately be better off without each other.

Other answers may surprise you. I recently developed some dental issues and was referred to a respected periodontist. Three seconds after I obeyed Dr. Shimoda's order to "open wide" he stated with complete confidence, "You grind your teeth at night."

I closed my mouth. "What do you mean I grind my teeth? How do *you* know?" I was incredulous. How could that possibly be true? How could *I* not know I grind my teeth all night? Seriously, if I was a nightly teeth grinder wouldn't someone lying next to me in bed have mentioned it in the last 35 years?

Dr. Shimoda enlightened me. "Well, first of all, I know because the sides of your tongue are frayed. You grind so hard you bite your tongue all night long."

A little voice in my head whispered, "Actually you've been biting your tongue your whole life... and not just at night."

The little voice was right. Like many women of my generation I did have a lifelong habit of biting my tongue, not just when I slept--- but when I was wide-awake. Even worse, sometimes I said yes when I meant no. This dental visit was a wakeup call for me. I knew it was time to quit this unhealthy pattern and set a new policy.

So (with the help of a mouth guard that I wear at night) I no longer bite my tongue like I used to. I speak up. I've quit saying yes when the correct answer is, "No, thank you." I've come to understand that the word "no" is a complete sentence. *No.* No is a sacred answer. No one ever died from hearing the word no. (But I suspect many have died from the stress of uttering too many yeses.)

To take the next step we must be willing to say no to both ourselves and to others. We might have to practice the words rolling off our tongues but with enough repetitions we can confidently state, "Nope, don't want to, don't need to, not going to," more often, and with only an occasional twinge of guilt. In a few instances, "Hell, no!" may be the more accurate and appropriate response.

Sam Horn, author of *Tongue Fu: How to Deflect, Disarm, and Diffuse Any Verbal Conflict,* offers this suggestion to make swallowing the pill of "no" easier for everyone. When you want to say no, add the phrase, "I wish I could." It acknowledges that you are not rejecting the person or their request. Sam coaches, "We can't always give people what they want, but we can give them our concern."

Knowing how to say no means we can also turn down seemingly "great" opportunities

> In time we come to recognize that the more we authentically say no, the more our yes will have real impact.

because they do not match our intentions. (That job change that means a little more money, but a lot more travel, plus nights and weekends...that sleek new car that requires higher monthly insurance payments...that save-the-date destination wedding of the daughter of a former colleague you haven't seen in months that you really, really don't want to commit to...) In time we come to recognize that the more we authentically say no, the more our yes will have real impact.

Saying no will at times mean speaking up and insisting we be heard. We may have to quit being so polite. Perhaps we should all consider embracing former Secretary of State Madeline Albright's wisdom that, when asked what one piece of advice she'd give women, she replied: *Interrupt.*

According to my mail, I am not the only one who sees the wisdom of speaking up, and it is not just women who feel this way. One man wrote, "I plan to quit dancing around my 15-year-old son's feelings about his mom's and my divorce and my subsequent remarriage and ask him to face them head on. It's been five years since the divorce and almost two years since I remarried. In an effort to stay connected I have called him or sent an email almost every day since the divorce. He has been distant since I remarried and that is now taking a toll on all the relationships. I won't quit calling but I will quit avoiding the tough subjects and get things out into the open!"

The answer to what to quit is *everything that is not in line with your intention.* Whether that becomes immediately obvious or requires serious introspection doesn't matter. Stick with it and the answer to this all-important question will become evident.

Be Forewarned

Let me give you a heads-up. When we set a clear intention, whatever is in the way of that desire will automatically come up for review. For example, if you've decided to leave a love relationship that you know is wrong for you, things will pop up to test your decision. One man, who had decided to tell his girlfriend that he could not make a commitment to her, told me he was looking for the instruction manual on how to fix the garbage disposal when he came across the romantic card she'd had sent him a year earlier. He asked, "How did her card get in *that* file?" He said, "After reading her loving sentiments I spent the rest of the day wondering if I really wanted to break up with her. Finding her card was a real test for me."

For women, "should I or shouldn't I?" plays out something like this: Just when you think you are finally healed you *will* run into your ex, on the day you have not showered because you have been working in the yard all day and just ran to the grocery store to get trash bags. Your former flame will, of course, be perfectly coifed and dressed for a supermodeling assignment on the French Riviera. "Your song" will play on the radio, and if not that one, every "Breaking Up is Hard to Do" song ever composed will play on whatever station you flip to.

And whether you are male or female: Start to date someone else, and without warning your ex will text you like he or she is sending SOS messages from a deserted island. Observe your emotional and physiological response and honor whatever it is. Give yourself credit for quitting what was never going to work out and be compassionate because the song is right: Breaking up *is* hard to do.

The tests of will may seem unrelenting. If you have set an intention to lose weight, dinner invitations will pour in. The reclusive neighbor you haven't spoken to in six months will unexpectedly pop over with her homemade Death by Chocolate pie topped with melted marshmallows. She'll insist you sit down right now and eat a big piece while she hovers over you waiting for your rave review. I can practically guarantee that if you decide you need some more time for yourself, needy relatives wanting to visit will come out of the woodwork like hungry termites searching for their next meal. Plan to leave your corporate position to start your own business, and the next week you'll receive a glowing performance evaluation, a raise and a big bonus with hints of a promotion. The Universe will be asking whether or not you are serious about your stated desires. Be ready with your answer.

A Really Hard One to Quit

When the topic for review is "friends" we squirm. Most of us have taken to heart the refrain in the Girl Scout song, "Make new friends but keep the old. One is silver and the other gold." But chances are when you decide what to quit in order to move forward some people will inevitably be left behind, temporarily or permanently, for a host of valid reasons. Some friends we simply outgrow, while others no longer support our vision. Our new path may move us geographically or philosophically a long way away. We also may have friends who are, if we are frank with ourselves, needy, toxic, energy-sucking people that make us feel like we are circling the drain whenever we are around them.

> When we see ourselves as grateful, healthy, and passionate with a higher vision for our lives we raise the bar for everyone.

Most business partnerships benefit from having a detailed, mutually agreed upon exit strategy, preferably planned before the names appear on the dotted lines. How much easier it might be if we had one for every friendship we enter, a sort of prenuptial agreement for the masses. But it doesn't work that way and letting a friendship lapse can feel like doing surgery with the jagged edge of a broken pop bottle.

But the choice to quit a friendship can actually benefit both parties. When we decide to shift away from our obvious need to be desperately needed, our willingness to be treated with disrespect and our symbiotic agreement to give away energy, we open up a whole new realm of possibilities for all concerned. When we see ourselves as grateful, healthy, and passionate with a higher vision for our lives we raise the bar for everyone.

Finding the Time

In order to find the time to set intentions and make good on them you will probably need to get out the machete and hack away at your work and social calendar. Many of us have the habit of seeing an open slot and compulsively filling it. In mathematics when we add and add and add without stopping the result is called infinity. In life when we add and add and add without stopping it is called insanity. Something's gotta give.

Could you quit 20 minutes a day of Facebook? What might you accomplish in that two hours and 20 minutes a week? Could you reassign chores at home, carpool, or quit the book club or tennis round robin that is more of a burdensome habit than a delight? Could you take a one month sabbatical from your volunteer activities and use the time to focus on your new direction? A commitment to change requires just that: commitment. You will need to carve out time, resources and (probably) money.

I can hear the push back: "I am so busy. I really have no idea how I will create more time." "But I have a limited budget." "I don't know where to find the resources I would need." I understand. When we are not sure how to make the changes we must reaffirm what it is we want. Those quarks are somehow listening and who knows what will disappear from our calendar or show up unexpectedly just by being crystal clear that we are ready to make a move. Sign up for an exercise class and the teenager next door will stop by asking for an after-school babysitting job, making it easier for you to find the time to go regularly. Decide to go back to college and small scholarships and part-time jobs may mysteriously appear. Send out a wish for a new passion and family friends will buy a boat and want you to join them at the lake. Make a commitment to more of what you want and it just might show up without too much effort at all on your part. Your major contribution may simply be a decision to make room for it when it arrives--and that will require quitting the time commitments that are in the way.

When to Quit

Many of us know what to quit but balk at taking the next step because we're not sure when to quit. So we wait to get sick or fired, fed up or emotionally damaged. We procrastinate until it is too late to sell the business or save our liver. Some of us wait until we hear ourselves scream, "I can't take it anymore!" and we finally hit rock bottom. We stay in toxic situations where we feel under-appreciated, overworked or disrespected because we badly need the health insurance and as a result, we badly need the health insurance. One of my friends described his insane reluctance to resign from his obsolete job by saying, "I was riding the horse when it fell down and died. The steam was rising from its carcass but I was still sitting in the saddle, yelling 'Giddy-up.'" It is not always true, but often the time to quit is sooner than we're willing to admit.

Still, letting someone or something go has its own time. If it feels like you are pushing, forcing and dragging, then "inquire within" again for the source of the resistance. As the seers say, that's where the answers lie. Once you get those answers you will have the information you need to decide whether to wait or make a plan to quit now.

How to Quit

Quit as consciously, confidently and gracefully as you can and in a style that is consistent with your highest values. You might decide to quit immediately. My all-time favorite anti-smoking campaign slogan is "Cold Turkey is Better Than Dead Duck." You might quit in stages, face to face, in a letter, on Skype, or in the therapist's office. You might need your best friend, a career counselor, Jenny Craig or Dr. Phil every day at three p.m. *Whatever your plan, see yourself succeeding.*

Sometimes it's the small adjustments that have the most impact. One woman told me that she took a step in the *right* direction by simply looking in a *different* direction. She loved huge family gatherings, especially at the holidays, but after her brother got married he started spending those days with his wife's family. As a result she felt that something was missing from her beloved holiday. She said, "I was focused on the fact that I was not invited to my brother's home for a big family holiday celebration. One day I realized I just needed to adjust my view. When I took my gaze off the 'problem' and looked at it from a slightly different angle I discovered I had what I wanted all along. I married into it! I've spent wonderful holidays with my husband's large, loving family for more than 25 years. I also had lots of meaningful time with my own family at other times of the year." Once she quit defining what the date and décor had to be for her to feel happy, she was.

It's important to remember something that we wish wasn't true: *Lasting change often takes multiple attempts.*

On average a smoker will have tried to stop more than four times before finally kicking the nicotine addiction. The only membership requirement to join AA is a desire to quit. Yet recovering alcoholics may go to meetings for the rest of their lives. There are, allegedly, 50 ways to leave your lover. You may need to try out several of them before you are successful.

> We stay in toxic situations where we feel under-appreciated, over-worked or disrespected because we badly need the health insurance, and as a result, we badly need the health insurance.

Have faith that as you say yes to the next step there's a way to quit and you will figure it out.

Why You Are Quitting

I believe you quit for two main reasons. First, you quit because "it" is in the way of you getting what you really want. If you get honest with yourself you can admit that what used to work doesn't anymore, as much as you wish it would. Setting an intention causes you to expand and that is why you get that itchy, claustrophobic, nauseous feeling that you wish would go away, but won't. The symptoms simply mean you need room to grow. You've sprouted wings and the old cocoon doesn't feel so good anymore. Maybe you can't explain it to anyone but you can hear your inner voice playing "Seventy-Six Trombones" to get your attention. You understand you just no longer fit.

Secondly, you quit because, paradoxically, while the process might be very difficult in the short run, it almost always makes life easier in the long run. The dance moves flow infinitely better when I stop flapping my arms. An under-arm turn is way easier when I don't duck. Quitting is like taking off a leaden coat before you decide to scale the mountain.

Taking a Stand

A few times a year I hold transformational women's retreats in Kauai. The first morning I ask my guests to journal about the concept of quitting. One of my attendees, Lynn, offered her journal entry that insightfully describes how making the difficult decision to quit can create ease:

In my family I have always taken on the role of 'Family Peacemaker.' I am not certain whether I was assigned this role or just self-selected but that is what I did for over 50 years. I was never happy in that role and often found myself to be under-appreciated without a voice of my own.

There came a time when lots of financial decisions had to be made regarding my mother. I am the only sibling or sibling in-law to live away from the family. Therefore, many decisions were being made with an expectation that I would participate, but without a voice. Initially I found myself falling, once again, into the peacemaker role as I wanted my mother to be happy and I certainly didn't want the family to be disappointed in me if I didn't agree with their choices. Not being local had its benefits and difficulties but I would say it was mostly the latter. There was a building project involved and I was not asked to participate in decisions nor did I agree with the financial decisions being made that would ultimately cost me money.

Fifty plus years of agreeing to keep the peace came bubbling up and something told me that it was time to take a stand. The decision to quit this role was a very difficult one.... What would they think of me?... They were my family – how could I disappoint?... What would my mother think? It was time to quit this role and have my voice heard. I took the plunge but it was very difficult. For the first time I stood my ground with my brother and sister-in-law and they began to view me in a different light. I won't say it was easy and this decision to quit changed my family relationships forever.

The interesting thing is that once I made the decision to quit the peacemaker role and go along with everyone else I had a new sense of myself. It didn't happen overnight but after a few years I noticed that my relationship with family became more relaxed as I let things flow rather than trying to force them to happen in the way I thought they should for everyone to be happy.

Lynn beautifully illustrates that making a simple decision to change how she viewed herself caused a domino effect in her family. Instead of asking her family to quit treating her in a certain way, she simply quit participating as usual in the family dynamics, and things got easier for everyone.

Case in Point: More than Meets the Eye

Joan Brock will never forget the day before her thirty-second birthday. She led a happy, healthy life with her husband Joe and their three-year-old daughter Joy. Joan and Joe had deeply satisfying careers together at the Iowa Braille and Sight Saving School, he as the director of leisure and recreational training and she as the liaison between dorm parents and classroom teachers.

That pre-birthday morning Joan went to the dresser drawer to find Joy's socks to get her ready for school. "Pumpkin, what happened to your pink socks?"

"There they are, Mommy. They're in the corner--lots of them."

Joan followed the direction of Joy's finger. "But those are white."

Joy sighed impatiently. "Oh, Mommy, they're pink, pink, pink, like my pants."

Joan picked up the pair and examined it closely under the Winnie the Pooh lamp. There was no trace of color at all.

As the day wore on, Joan's vision continued to worsen. In the ladies' room she looked in the mirror and saw a pale, wan complexion. She pulled out her compact and her hand froze. The blush looked as white as talcum powder. Later she tripped over a curbside mound of snow in the bright sunlight. By the end of day she was wearing sunglasses because the office lights made her squint. Hearing about her visual difficulties a colleague at school gave her a special magnifying device resembling a baseball, but flattened at the top and bottom. It would magnify letters five-fold. After work Joan stole away to the deserted library, took a large-print book to a corner desk and placed the device on the page. *She could not make out a single letter.*

In her bestselling book, *More Than Meets the Eye*, Joan writes, "A brutal truth hit me with a crushing impact. My central vision was all but gone. Many of the partially blind children at my school could see better than I could now see. 'Oh God! Oh God!' I cried in the silent library."

Two weeks later at the University of Iowa her doctor delivered a diagnosis Joan had been dreading: she had a rare autoimmune disorder. "The deterioration of your eyesight is irreversible," he explained.

Without any warning, Joan had gone blind in three weeks.

Joan adjusted. If you can use the word *luckily*, as a teacher of the blind she was well versed in many of the skills she would need to cope and she was married to a man who was trained in those same skills. I wish I could tell you that the happy ending begins here. In a twist of tragic irony, Joe developed severe headaches, and the same doctor who diagnosed Joan gave Joe his bad news: cancer of the sinuses. The required radical surgery meant removing Joe's right eye. Sitting on the exam table Joe turned to Joan and said, "Honey, we can manage on one working eye, can't we?"

Despite aggressive chemotherapy the cancer grew. After a gallant seven month fight Joe lost his life.

"And that is when," Joan says, "I really went blind."

"It was a double loss. I had all the pain of losing my spouse and now I was faced with reality. Before this I had relied on Joe and on the school, but I realized I hadn't really faced the brutal truth of my blindness until now. How would I shop, pay the bills, raise a child alone, get insurance? My list of concerns was endless."

In less than a year Joan's life had been upended in the most unthinkable ways. The mother of a seven-year-old, she was blind, widowed, unemployed, and feeling unemployable. How on earth was she going to take her *next step* when she literally could not see where she was going?

Now For That Happy Ending

I met Joan years later. She's a gorgeous, long-legged blond bombshell, blissfully married to her husband of 20 years, a hunka hunka burning love, Jim Brock. Joan is a wildly successful motivational speaker and author, and her life story has been made into a TV movie.

I asked her, "So, Joan, tell me. You took the next step so courageously. What did you have to quit to create such a wonderful life for yourself?"

"Well, first I had to quit driving," she quipped with her wicked sense of humor.

She must have sensed the dirty look I shot her. She laughed. "Okay, I'll be serious. You're right. Before I could take the next step there were lots of things I needed to quit.

"When Joe died I had to quit four years of denial. I had to acknowledge that I could not live as a sighted woman. I had to decide to see in a different way.

"Mary, I am generally a very positive person but I had to quit feeling sorry for myself. When I lived through Joe's terrible drama with him it gave me perspective. I thought, 'Holy crap, I have nothing to complain about. Nothing about my condition is important.'

"That helped. When you quit focusing on yourself and you help others, you heal. I had a new purpose. This helped me go forward as a productive woman.

"But the biggest challenge was I had to quit my former life. I moved back to California and I said goodbye to my friends, colleagues and community, my home, and my career.

"And then I had to quit letting the world roll over me. It was when I finally said, 'ENOUGH!' that I recognized how fiercely independent I was and how determined I was to find my way. The vision of my life was not gone. The hopes and dreams were still there.

"I quit wishing it were different. That is such a revolving door. It's been 28 years, nearly half my life spent in darkness. I will tell you it still frustrates me to no end. I wanted to see my daughter walk down the aisle as a beautiful bride a few years ago. But I do not let that take me into despair. I live with hope."

Over the years I've had the good fortune to witness how graciously and humorously Joan has quit feeling sorry for herself. She often puts others at ease, for example, by greeting the restaurant hostess with a smile and a request for a table with a view. I notoriously have no sense of direction so she likes to jokingly complain that I make a very poor seeing-eye dog and then she suggests that I follow *her* back to our hotel room. With my navigation skills she says I am lucky to have her. And I agree. Very lucky indeed.

Tell Me Why Again—and What, When and How

Why is it so imperative that we quit in order to take the next step? It depends on whom you ask. The business experts argue that strategic quitting is smart management. Why pour precious resources--time, money and a creative workforce--into something that is not going to catapult you to the top? The spiritual teachers believe quitting creates a vacuum that the Universe can quickly fill with what you really want. The Feng Shui masters say quitting clears an energy path, opening up the flow of chi. Mystics say quitting allows you to see the answers through the mist and fog. And there are others who say quitting dissolves cellulite, eliminates unwanted hair, and raises your odds of winning the lottery. Whatever. I say "just quit."

Getting rid of things that are not the dance takes focus and a willingness to let go of the old, comfortable, been-like-a-family-to me habits, beliefs, people, things and boxes of stuff that have been in the basement since you first moved in. (Gee, was that really 16 years ago?)

You will often wonder, "Should I quit now or later?" As the saying goes, the time to buy an antique is when you see it. The same advice applies to quitting. You will know when.

The process can be scary, unpleasant, and painfully awkward. It can also be unbelievably liberating, exhilarating and profitable. Mostly it's just necessary because it blocks what you really want. I've never met anyone who could not answer the question, "What did you have to quit to get where you are now?" Getting rid of impediments will always be a prerequisite to moving forward.

If you are starting to get a rash, I understand. In the short run it probably is easier not to rock the marital boat, speak up at the PTA meeting or emphatically tell your father no. For right now holding your chair down at work may sound infinitely more palatable than looking for a job in a field you feel newly passionate about. But we all know that denying the truth hardly ever works out well in the long run.

Opportunity may knock only once but temptation leans on the doorbell.

So quit already. Quit repeat offenders, the ones you find lurking behind well-meaningness. Quit the things you now know your mother was right about all along. Quit some friendships so you can both spend time with people who are better suited to you. And when the review process inevitably begins, remember this anonymous truism: Opportunity may knock only once but temptation leans on the doorbell. You will be seduced with advice that tells you to just keep things the way they are. Stay focused on the prize. You can do this.

Years from now, when you say to your friends, "Let me tell you about the time I quit..." you will see in your story that your actions sprang from a clear intention and led you to a good life in ways you probably never expected. And you will be grateful that you knew that winners do indeed quit.

Accepting the Invitation

Dear Mary,

A few years ago I determined I was going to go to law school. To that end I started researching and reviewing the LSAT test schedule. At that time I was in a job where I traveled weekly and I arranged to take the test at a location that coordinated with my schedule. I was all set—or so I thought. What I didn't do was study.

The day came and I sat the exam and was miserable. I knew I wasn't prepared for such a major test, and on top of that I was stressed about "fitting it in" between the demands of the job that I was actually in town for. My upbringing did not allow me to "quit" so I stuck it out and, not surprisingly, did quite badly. Ultimately, I did not go to law school for a variety of reasons, but one of them was definitely the fact that my low LSAT scores limited my choice of schools.

Fast-forward a year or two and my husband decides he wants to go to law school. I helped him sign up for the LSAT test offered in our hometown and he studied diligently until the date came. After about an hour and a half he was home. This was not long enough to have completed the over three-hour exam. I asked him what happened because in my mind they would have had to cancel the test for him to have been finished so early. He said that he didn't feel good about how he was doing so he surrendered his test and left. I was FURIOUS! I couldn't believe he'd "quit." I started getting very smug about how I had at least hung in there and did not let my sense of how "good" I felt influence my ability to finish the task at hand and added loads of other condescending comments in that vein.

He patiently explained to me that the rules of the LSAT counted all scores cumulatively. If you take the test multiple times the scores are averaged into a single LSAT score submitted to the law school(s) where you apply. Those same rules allowed you to exit the exam prior to completion and render no score, which didn't count, in the cumulative score. So it actually made better sense statistically to quit if you thought you weren't going to do well rather than turn in a low score and have to try and raise it by taking subsequent tests. He finished by pointing out that I had done so much research on the LSAT exam he thought I would've known that.

I was so angry (but not at my husband) because I DID KNOW THAT. It had been so ingrained in me that quitting was bad that I had actually done harm to my chances of getting into law school because I could not quit even though it made better sense to do so. I learned a great deal about the value of quitting and listening to my gut reaction.

This lesson hits home.

--Renee Bates

THE LESSON: *QUIT*

Know what to quit.
Know when to quit.
Know how to quit.
Know why you are quitting.
Then just quit.

Take Your Next Step

What do you need to quit?

Chapter Three

Embrace Ambiguity

In Zen Buddhism, there's a concept called 'beginner's mind.' They say that the mind should be like an empty rice bowl. If it's already full the Universe can't fill it. If it's empty, it has room to receive. This means that when we think we have things already figured out, we're not teachable. Genuine insight can't dawn on a mind that's not open to receive it. In the Christic tradition, this is the meaning of 'becoming as a little child.' Little children don't think they know what things mean. In fact, they know they don't know.

--Marianne Williamson

My ballroom studio holds a dance party every Friday night. Students can come for free and the instructors attend as well. After a few weeks of lessons, I decided this party would be a good way for me to get in some practice. Little did I know I was about to get practice of an entirely different kind.

I arrived at the studio feeling like a freshman at the senior prom, but excited at the prospect of dancing the night away. About 25 students milled around waiting for the music to start. Much to my delight, I counted a nearly equal number of leaders and followers. The odds of doing lots of dancing looked good. I slipped on my shoes and sat down on one of the chairs at the far end of the ballroom, and patiently waited for an invitation to dance.

After 30 minutes I was still sitting there by myself, with most everyone else partnered and moving to the music. Finally a man invited me onto the floor as a foxtrot tune began to play. I had just a few foxtrot lessons under my belt and although I tried my best, the poor guy basically had to drag me around the floor. We'd have had more fun listening to a forty-five minute drum solo. He politely escorted me back to my chair. I sat back down for another half hour, again, waiting for my next invitation.

At most dances I'd been to in my life, the boys chose the most popular or prettiest or curviest girls first and often. Not true at this party. The leaders wanted to dance with the most skilled followers, even if the leaders themselves were not as talented. It didn't matter how sexy your legs *looked*. It mattered how well they *danced*.

I understood this reasoning. As an athletic youngster I usually served as the captain of the team, picking the players, and if I was not the captain then I was always selected for a team within the first few rounds. Being drafted last was new to me.

I must give the men credit where credit is due. They

were compassionate and they gave me a shot. One guy even stopped to show me how to perform *my* steps. Another man asked me to do the East Coast swing, a high-energy, jive-like dance. (Think Little Ritchie at the Hop.) Again, I tried my best, attempting to "triple step, triple step, rock step" fast enough to keep up with my much more proficient leader. Unfortunately, there was clearly a major disconnect between what my mind was telling my body to do and what physically occurred on the dance floor. Generously this kind gentleman stuck it out with me until the end of the song. Bless his heart.

It is okay not to know.

I did not get asked to dance again.

I lay in bed that night going over what had just happened and what it meant. What it meant had been made crystal clear: If I was going to learn to dance, I'd need to wrap my arms around Captain Kirk and boldly go where I'd never been before. I was going to have to get real comfortable with not knowing much of anything for a while. This information had not appeared anywhere in the studio's brochure, not even in the fine print on the last page.

So I made a commitment that night to get as comfortable as I could with uncertainty. I had set up house in Ihavenoide-awhatIamdoingville, and I promised myself that even when I got really scared, lost, frustrated, embarrassed, bored, dejected or God only knows what other emotions, I would not pack up and move out in the middle of the night. I'd stick around, meet the neighbors, hang some curtains and find the closest grocery store. I wanted to be part of this neighborhood.

Learning to dance forced me to understand that it is okay not to know. When we get to the party we don't know for sure if, when, or with whom we'll dance, what song will play, or what leads we'll receive. Every leader has his own style. The invitation is essentially, "Would you like to spend the next several minutes with me having no idea exactly what will happen?"

We must accept that we can only dance one movement, one moment, at a time. We really can't know anything past that. Perhaps this is what Eckhart Tolle, author of *A New Earth* meant when he wrote:

> Stepping forward meant I would have to be willing to calmly step in place and just wait in the dark.

"When you are on a journey, it is certainly helpful to know where you are going or at least the general direction in which you are moving, but don't forget: the only thing that is ultimately real about your journey is the step that you are taking at this moment. That's all there ever is."

The lesson I learned at the practice party: To dance is to embrace ambiguity.

I don't remember having to embrace ambiguity as an eight-year-old in tap shoes, probably because as a child I comfortably swam in a sea of it as a way of life. Most kids and young people just do. Of course, I'm still swimming in that same ocean now but I have tamped down that truth so I can keep anxiety at bay, pretending that I am in control and always know what to do.

I went home from the dance party wiser. I understood that stepping forward meant I would have to be willing to calmly step in place and just wait in the dark. In the Tao Te Ching, the classic manual on the art of living, author Lao-tzu wrote, "Do you have the patience to wait till your mud settles and the water is clear? Can you remain unmoving till the right action arises by itself?" When I read this I fantasized about the possibility that in 500 BC Lao-Tzu, too, might have gained this bit of wisdom as he learned to ballroom dance.

Just Hanging Out There

By definition our decision to take the next step in life places us in a position of not knowing. We've quit, which cleaned out a space in our lives and we want to know what will take its place, what will happen next, what will life be like now. What are we supposed to do? How can we guarantee success? What's the best, fastest, least expensive way to get what we want? We need, want, and plead for answers. *Right now.*

The answer to most of those questions? *Wait and see.* Cozy up to not knowing for a while. Yes, easier said than done. Believe me, I get that. When you crave some kind of forward momentum, embracing ambiguity can sound as appealing as rolling around naked in poison ivy. Unless we spend our days chanting in a hilltop monastery, we rarely wake up saying, "Boy, I just have no idea what's going on. I'm not at all sure what direction to take but I'm so at peace with all that." No, our anxiety builds and we feel compelled to do something, *anything*. We want a concrete plan so that we can avoid facing the truth that, frankly, we haven't a clue where to even begin. To cope, we make up imaginary deadlines. We decide we have to have a job by March 14 or two thousand dollars by the end of the month or the person we met online must call back by four o'clock on Tuesday. We demand a candle, a torch, a flashlight - something to hold onto so we can pierce the darkness that obscures our future and see what's in store for us.

Confusion Endurance
(It's not for the faint of heart)

Leonardo da Vinci, perhaps the greatest genius of all time, believed his ability to embrace uncertainty, ambiguity and paradox was one of the secrets to his brilliance. He called this ability *sfumato*, meaning, "turned to mist" or "going up in smoke."

The sfumato principle encourages us to cultivate what da Vinci called "**confusion endurance,**" **an ability to thrive in the tension of not knowing.** Michael Gelb, author of *How to Think Like Leonardo da Vinci* wrote, "Keeping your mind open in the face of uncertainty is the single most powerful secret of unleashing your creative potential." As we all know unleashed creative potential is a handy thing to have lying around the house when you own real estate in Ihavenoideawhatiamdoingville.

Sometimes we happily sign up for the new adventure and enjoy the juicy unknown, but frequently we are thrown into it seemingly out of nowhere with a force so hard we feel shaken and dazed. We come to in a very foreign place that is uncomfortable or dicey or hurts like hell. Ambiguity can scare us half to death, like a crazy nightmare where we are clinging to a frayed rope bridge that is swaying over a raging river full of two-headed crocodiles. When we open our eyes in the morning our stomachs ache, our hearts race, and our palms grow sweaty. The nightmare is over, but we've just realized that we're as confused and unsure this morning as we were last night.

Don't be surprised at the repressed emotion that may bubble up to the surface as you tango with confusion endurance. You could experience moments of depression, despair, anxiety or panic. I remember a time when I was in this ambiguous phase and was so angry I had to fight off an intense irrational urge to grab a ski mask and knock off a couple of liquor stores. When I seem to be losing it I am comforted by author Julia Cameron's words, "At first flush, going *sane* feels just like going crazy."

This emotional intensity often leads to awareness, which is the perfect place to live because then we have a choice. We can choose fear, which is the certainty that nothing is going to work out--or faith, the certainty that it will work out just fine somehow or another, all in divine order.

In this space of awareness we can open the door to all the ideas, solutions, and exciting opportunities that are incubating, which is what da Vinci did. We can invite them in for a cup of tea or a highball. We can tell them to put their feet up and relax, that they needn't rush. We can agree to receive their answers in the perfect time. Brilliant ideas and new opportunities have no relationship to time. They could appear in a nanosecond or on the Queen Mary. But they do eventually show up if we are willing to get still, and listen intently as we ask them to talk to us.

I remember when a friend started her new job with a famous international apparel company. Just 22 years old, with a college degree but not much business experience, she was put in charge of marketing socks. In her first week of employment she was asked to meet with her boss and her boss's boss and present a plan for quickly selling 43,000 pairs of last year's stock. She called me, totally lost about how to solve this problem and laughed, "The most fascinating part of all this is *they think I know*!" But she hung in there, buoyed by the fact that her superiors had faith in her even when she knew she had no immediate plan for successfully meeting this challenge. She flailed a bit for sure, but after a while she devised some fairly ingenious marketing methods, sold all the stock, and went on to many more professional successes.

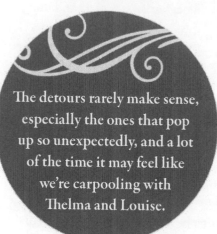

The detours rarely make sense, especially the ones that pop up so unexpectedly, and a lot of the time it may feel like we're carpooling with Thelma and Louise.

When we develop a high tolerance for uncertainty we gain a deeper understanding that life is not a straight line. The detours rarely make sense, especially the ones that pop up so unexpectedly, and a lot of the time it may feel like we're carpooling with Thelma and Louise. But when we step back just a little we do see that life is a circle, that we're not going to stay lost forever. We will find our way.

Confusion Endurance at Its Best

I had the wonderful honor of meeting the pilot of the "Miracle on the Hudson," Chesley B. Sullenberger III, at a private reception at the United States Air Force Academy. It was the summer after the "incident," which is how he described landing his commercial airplane on a river to his wife when he called her from the lifeboat. Sully is a charming, humble, good-hearted man. And obviously, one helluvan aviator.

A 1973 graduate of the Air Force Academy, Captain Sullenberger regaled the 2700 admiring cadets in Arnold Hall Theater that evening with many inspirational stories. The story that stopped me, however, was his description of the actual water landing. As I listened to his remarks I realized his heroic feat was a miracle not only because 155 people lived to tell about it. It was a dramatic example of two airline pilots who were obviously masters of confusion endurance. The transcripts of their conversations with each other and with the control tower revealed unbelievably calm, professional, and to the point communication. DaVinci would have been very impressed.

From the time Sully said, "Birds," as a flock of geese covered his cockpit windshield, to the moment he was floating on the river, only 209 seconds had passed. Moments before landing Captain Sullenberger turned to his co-pilot and asked, "Got any ideas?" To which first officer Jeff Skiles calmly replied, "Actually, not."

Well why would he? While pilots do go through extensive "ditching" training, they do not practice water landings via a simulator like they do other maneuvers. The two men had over 40,000 hours of flying time between them so this was not their first rodeo, but on the other hand, neither of them had ever done a swan dive in an Airbus A320 and neither had hardly any other pilots alive at the time.

Alrighty then. We have us a serious case of ambiguity. And yes, the 77 years of combined experience of the flight attendants, the skills and professionalism of the air traffic controller and the ferryboat rescuers, along with the bravery of the passengers, played a huge role in averting disaster. I have to conclude, however, that confusion endurance on everyone's part was a vitally important piece of this miracle.

If you think you are a little uncomfortable with not knowing how things are going to turn out, imagine these pilots' emotions as they experienced the equivalent of being in an elevator dropping two floors a second. Embracing ambiguity does not mean you do absolutely nothing. Au contraire. These men were very busy, totally focused on the task at hand. It does mean you accept not knowing, watch for answers as they appear and react accordingly.

At dinner on the night we met, Sully told me that seconds after the plane came to a rest on the icy river, he and co-pilot Skiles turned to each other and simultaneously said exactly the same words, "Well, that wasn't as bad as I thought."

It immediately struck me that we all have those moments when we fear something is going to be awful, so we worry, resist, procrastinate, get scared or totally freaked out, only to admit after we actually do it, that well, it wasn't as bad as we thought. Hanging out in the unknown, what my friend calls "living between the parentheses," demands that we continue to function even when we have no ideas, even when we fear the worst.

All of us experience this phenomenon in our own lives, albeit less dramatically. Take dieting, for example. Dr. Judith Beck, world-expert cognitive therapist and author of the terrific book, *The Beck Diet Solution*, offers this technique for losing weight: *Practice hunger tolerance.* It turns out hunger is not an emergency. In fact, if you wait a while the hunger and craving may even pass. People have actually gone for more than a week without eating and haven't died. So skipping that frosted brownie, the carton of chocolate chip-cookie dough ice cream, or the bag of potato chips that's calling your name won't kill you, and waiting out the craving for 30 minutes is probably not going to be as bad as you think.

A few weeks ago I bought the P90X exercise program featuring 12 extreme kick-your-butt DVDs. For a lifetime exerciser this is the hardest thing I have ever attempted. And I absolutely love it.

Still, every morning I resist going downstairs to do that day's work out. So I say to myself, "It's not going to be as bad as I think." And it never is and I am always glad I did it.

In 10 weeks I lost 7 pounds and 3 inches off my waist using Sully's words.

Consider using this technique when you have no idea what to do next, in part because you fear the worst. Whether it's stalling on your tax preparation, dreading a vacation with the in-laws, receiving a performance review or making the telephone call you've been avoiding, chances are it's just like landing a plane on the Hudson.

Embrace ambiguity. It's not going to be as bad as you think.

Case in Point: Catching the Trade Winds

My son, Nick, used the strategy of embracing ambiguity after he graduated from college with a degree in journalism in 2009. In the midst of the worldwide economic downturn, seasoned journalists and cub reporters alike were having trouble finding work in their field. So Nick decided to go to Asia and get a job teaching English. However, after weeks of researching and applying online for jobs in Japan, Korea, China and Taiwan, he had no offers.

One morning he strolled into the kitchen, made himself some toast with strawberry jelly, poured a glass of milk and plopped down beside me at the breakfast counter. Then, in the matter-of-fact way 23-year-old men announce to their mothers that they are leaving home, he said after a big gulp of milk, "By the way, I'm going to fly to Taiwan this week and knock on doors until I get a job. Now don't say anything. I know what you're thinking. 'Nick, this is not a good plan because you've never even been to Taiwan nor do you know anyone there. You also don't have a place to stay, nor have a job, *and* you can't read, write, or speak Taiwanese.'"

He put his arm around me and grinned. "I already know all that. So I just want to say, 'I love you, Mom. Don't worry. I'll be fine.'"

And he left.

And I worried.

Each week his family, friends and I lived vicariously through his blog postings. I have included some abbreviated excerpts, followed by a quote he often added from one of his favorite authors. As you will see, he has embraced the principle of sfumato and likes "going up in smoke."

September 8, 2009

The Beginning
Ah to be young and reckless

It didn't sink in until I stood at the opening of the international terminal at LAX as Japanese crackled over the intercom, and a throng of Filipinos zipped past me. Noticing that I was by far in the minority, I got that little fear in me. The good kind of fear—the kind that makes you stand on guard a touch more and notice the small things . . . the kind where the unknown—good or bad—makes life more exciting.

A smile percolated on my face in realizing how obscenely difficult, how disastrously fun, how unyieldingly ambiguous my new endeavor is and will be. I walked around the airport with this dumb sort of grin on my face, and it didn't change until I boarded my plane.

Now after traveling for days and finally arriving at my hostel, I am content. Content in that I made my intention to get here and am now faced with the all-too-soon question of "what now?" So much of my focus over the past few weeks has been to overcome the obstacles and get to the place. Now I am faced with the much larger task of how to stay here and eke my way through. But it's liberating, exciting, frightening, emboldening, nerve wracking, growing, fun, and a whole list of other adjectives.

"Twenty years from now you will be more disappointed by the things that you didn't do than by the ones you did do. So throw off the bowlines. Sail away from the safe harbor. Catch the trade winds in your sails. Explore. Dream. Discover."

--Mark Twain

September 10, 2009

Job Hunting
Ah, to be young, jobless and uncomfortable

Three of the people just at this hostel are looking for jobs teaching English in Taipei. A recruiter told me she did not see any jobs on the horizon. I would be put as number 40 on her waiting list. The market is saturated with Americans flying the coop from their economically-depressed homeland. But I'll try and keep on trying and if things don't pan out, I might try looking for a job in Korea.

I am still jobless and worried about it, have not taken a hot shower in three days, and realize that with my language skills it will take me fifteen minutes to buy a donut for breakfast this morning. But it's one of those things that looking back, I'll laugh and say, "I remember when I was 23 and just moved to Taiwan. Oh, I stayed in the worst place, and it took me forever to find a job and blah, blah, blah."

"The test of an adventure is that when you're in the middle of it, you say to yourself, 'Oh, now I've got myself into an awful mess; I wish I were sitting quietly at home.' And the sign that something's wrong with you is when you sit quietly at home wishing you were out having lots of adventure."

--Thornton Wilder

September 27, 2009

The job response has been dismal, but I am undeterred and the lack of response is not destroying my spirits but making my desire for a job that much greater. Come Monday, my efforts will double and I am confident it will all work out.

Nick's confidence was soon rewarded. He found both an apartment and a Canadian roommate, Aaron, who became his partner in crime. Then the big prize arrived:

October 10, 2009

Ah, to be young and gainfully employed

I sat on the train fidgeting, on my way to give my big presentation to the big boss on my big day. I had to teach a demo where I incorporated the wide variety of skills thrown at me during the previous two weeks of job training. Arriving at the school, I poured over my notes for the presentation before finding a secluded room and practicing to the empty, non-criticizing, very kind chairs. After uproarious self-esteem-raising applause from my silent victims, I had to present my lecture to actual, thinking, judging, intelligent, interactive people.

My presentation focused around teaching the five senses. To illustrate them, I put a dead fish in a box, marked it "Magic Box" and had the students listen to a splash sound on my computer, and then I gave each student a little piece of fish on a toothpick to smell, touch, and taste. (In Taiwan raw fish is no biggie). After each sensory test the students would have to guess what was in the box. Is it bad that two of the three adult, fully cognizant, educated teachers did not guess fish? This is an accurate indicator of how well my teaching demo went. Dejected, I sat in a chair outside the classroom thinking, "Why the hell did I bring in a dead fish?"

Much to his surprise Nick got the job. As his best friend, David, wrote him in response, "Congrats on the job. All it took was a dead fish in a box."

From there Nick's adventures "escalated." The blogs opened with stories that began like this:

Ah, to be young, stupid, and bleeding

I touched my chin and looked down at my hand covered in blood...

And from another posting:

Ah, to be young and on an adventure

I directed the scooter around another fading patch of concrete road . . . I ran my scooter into another scooter only once and drove off the road into a ditch twice. Much to the dismay of my mother, I'm going to buy a motorcycle as soon as I can.

I quickly sent a threatening reply. "If you ever buy a motorcycle I will take every naked childhood photo I have of you (and some of them show *everything*) and post them on the Internet. In other words, please lie to me when you get your motorcycle."

The blogs now used words like *sucker punches, indoor wake boarding, perilous hiking, hotties* and *hangovers.* In massive denial I prayed that false bravado played a big role in his entries. I stopped sending copies of his blog posts to Grandma and Grandpa but his middle-aged uncles never missed an entry. They enjoyed imagining the thrill of living dangerously.

And then, five months after his arrival, Nick sent this entry:

February 4, 2010

Bye Taiwan

I have left Taiwan. Just writing the sentence gives me a little shiver of remorse that crawls up my spine, pinching every nerve along the way. It's disappointing. It's demoralizing. It sucks. Unfortunately, there was nothing else to do. I just finished battling round number five of tonsillitis and need to get the glands removed.

On Sunday I said good-bye to my apartment and my roommate. On Monday I quit my job. On Tuesday I found a plane ticket back home. On Wednesday I flew back to the States.

It's amazing how long it took to get set-up: Find a job, get an apartment, meet people. It took months. To see it all go away—three days.

Thank you, Taiwan ... For the good times ... For teaching me ... For scaring me ... For making me laugh ... For challenging me ... For keeping me on my toes ... For giving me an adventure ... For culture shock ...

For helping me become a man.

Thank you.

After a long two-day trip Nick was back home, "the place," Robert Frost wrote, "where, when you have to go there, they have to take you in." Although Nick was geographically back where he started he was in every other way in a totally different space. His choice to face his fears and make friends with ambiguity had expanded him in ways he never dreamed. And after a brief visit and a tonsillectomy, Nick packed his bags, and flew off again, youthfully and joyfully diving into the delicious unknown with a one-way ticket to China.

And as his dutiful mother, I worried.

Embracing ambiguity takes courage--courage to believe in both the necessity of being in the dark, and in the inevitability of the proverbial light at the end of the tunnel, even when, not only have you never seen a train on *these* tracks, you've never even seen *a train*. If you can find the courage the result is often more meaningful, exciting, exotic and of more value in ways you couldn't possibly imagine while you were sitting in the tunnel.

Accepting the Invitation

Dear Mary,

At 50 years of age I summoned the perspective and courage to take a serious look at my work situation and take a huge leap of faith. Suddenly I realized this life wasn't going to last forever, so I'd better pay close attention to how I was spending my precious time here.

Nevertheless, it was a long and painful process to arrive at the conclusion to quit my job. As much as I loved it initially, several mergers and illogical management changes had created a culture where I felt my options were to either stay and compromise my professional and personal integrity, or get out. Ultimately I chose to leave.

Because my work environment was so sick and crazy I first wondered if something was wrong with me. Concerned that I might be depressed, I went to a therapist. After listening to me for only thirty minutes, she observed that not only was I not depressed, I had a healthy energy for everything in my life except my career. The short version of her conclusion was, "It's not you. It's your job."

I knew I had to resign, but I had big questions. Would we be okay financially? I was making more money than I'd ever expected. Was I crazy to walk away from it? What would I do? How would both my partner and me not working affect our lives?

While I could run projections to answer the financial questions, it was impossible to truly answer the others. Still, I felt like I had no other choice if I wanted to be happy. So I leapt out into the unknown. I created a slogan for myself, "Choose

Life, Quit Now", which a friend put on a t-shirt for me, and I decided to walk away from the job.

Since my boss was based in another city I told him my decision by phone. My hand shook so hard when I picked up the receiver to dial that I knocked my bottled water over and had to hang up and clean up the mess before I could make the call. When I told him, I felt a weight was lifted off my shoulders.

I've never regretted my decision for one second, not even when the stock market began crashing the same month I quit. There have been adjustments, some anticipated and some not. My life has evolved over these six years in such wonderful ways and I wouldn't change a thing. I've replaced a hectic, stressful, high-paying job with time for yoga, tai chi, French and piano lessons, a book group, travel and growing beautiful gladiolas. (I never knew one flower from the other before). The part-time consulting work I do keeps me intellectually engaged and is magnificently rewarding because I'm using what I've learned to help other people. The whole process of leaping out into the unknown makes me gutsier. And that has helped me to continue taking steps in the direction I want to go and never look back.

--Donna Sorensen

THE LESSON: *EMBRACE AMBIGUITY*

Set up house in Ihavenoideawhat I amdoingville.
Wait.
It's not going to be as bad as you think.
Tap into the power of confusion endurance.
Listen and watch for the answers.

Take the Next Step

What are you most uncertain about?

Chapter Four

Get Disinhibited

The big question is whether you are going to be able to say a hearty yes to your adventure.

--Joseph Campbell

Rumba is a Spanish word whose translation is related to "party" and let me just say, boy, is it ever. I remember taking my first rumba lesson and thinking that "party" doesn't quite cover it. I spent the entire hour red-faced with sweaty palms, looking as if I'd been at an exceedingly wild party ending in the arrest of half the guests.

In ballroom competition there are two styles of rumba, the American and the International. The American rumba is the version the Puritans would have preferred if they'd been allowed to sway their hips, which I am pretty sure they weren't. If you are going to dance the rumba with your cousin, your boss's spouse or your child's college roommate make sure it's the *American* rumba.

Why? Because the international rumba is the lap dance of the ballroom dances. It is, as George Bernard Shaw wrote, "the vertical expression of a horizontal desire." The Latin music is slow, sultry and sensual. Think hot, sweaty nightclubs with tobacco leaf ceiling fans, dancers wearing crisp white cotton, in 1930s Havana, where this Cuban dance originated.

For you reality TV show aficionados you may remember watching professional dancer Derek Hough perform the rumba with his partner, swim suit supermodel Joanna Krupa, on ABC's "Dancing with the Stars." As I watched them, I felt the need to avert my eyes and thought perhaps it would be more appropriate if they just got a room. And yet, I will confess, I could not stop voyeuristically watching every erotic move. The instant their performance was over, Derek ran over to Joanna's fiancé who was sitting in the front row and shook his hand vigorously, in effect saying, "I hope you understand why I was groping your bride-to-be for the last two minutes on national television. I mean, come on, man, I didn't *want* to... I *had* to. It was the rumba."

My rumba lesson taught me a lot about how to take the next step in life. To do this dance right you have to get rid of self-consciousness, take risks and get in a sexy, passionate frame of mind, doing things you would not normally do in public. You have to really go for it in ways that initially feel uncomfortable and probably violate at least one or two of the Ten Commandments. In a word, to do this dance you have to *become disinhibited*. Disinhibition is defined as "unrestrained behavior resulting from a lessening or loss of inhibitions or a disregard of cultural restraints." Yep, that's the rumba.

Your Brain: Holding You Back, or Running Wild

Disinhibition is a necessary requirement for moving forward in life. To attain this condition we need to consider the brain.

My brain (and yours) has many outstanding qualities: It can instantly calculate the final purchase price of a half-off item reduced another 75 percent. It never gains weight. And in a little-discussed fact, it keeps me following the rules and adhering to cultural norms. It inhibits me from getting too wild and crazy for my own safety and for those around me.

Here's how it works: The frontal lobe of our brain houses what could be called our inhibition center. When we get up in the morning and decide to wear business clothes to the meeting instead of our much more comfortable plaid flannel pajamas and purple fuzzy slippers (or for that matter, going to the office stark naked) it is in large part thanks to our orbitofrontal cortex inhibiting us from making the comfier and less professionally acceptable choices. It stops our foot from pressing on the gas pedal when the devil on our shoulder dares us to run the red light. It's what tells (smart) men to answer their wives' proverbial question, "Do these pants make me look fat?" with an immediate, incredulous and emphatic, "Absolutely not!" A well-functioning inhibition center is a good thing to have.

There are several things that depress our inhibition center. Alcohol and drugs are the two biggies. An alcohol/drug-depressed inhibition center does not stop us when we decide it would be a great idea to text our boss at one in the morning to share some of our concerns about his work performance. A depressed center is a common cause of waking up in the morning and discovering you are lying next to a stranger whose name escapes you. It explains most karaoke performances.

Another primary cause of disinhibition is normal aging. Like all parts of the body, our frontal lobe atrophies as we grow older, making it function less effectively. Perhaps you've experienced this when Grandma unexpectedly blurts out to your sister, "You're looking a little chunky these days. How do you expect to catch a man, especially at *your* age?" Everyone may gasp, "Grandma!" but she probably didn't mean to be unkind. Her less active frontal cortex isn't firing those neurons like it used to, making her just a bit disinhibited, albeit much to your chagrin. Most people to whom I explain this phenomenon immediately feel relief and can forgive (and laugh with) their elders. If we live long enough we'll all no doubt take a turn at saying a "truth" no one wants to hear.

> Overriding your frontal cortex when it fires off its overprotective warnings can be very good for what ails you.

There is a wonderful flip side to this view of disinhibition. Overriding your frontal cortex when it fires off its overprotective, be-careful-watch-out-get-back-what-do-you-think-you-are-doing warnings can be very good for what ails you, keeping you young at heart and full of life. I learned about this up close when I had the pleasure of touring the

US one year, speaking at 150 retirement villages. Every speech was a love-in with these feisty senior citizens. During my program I asked them what they were passionate about, and among the many answers offered they always included "dance" and "sex" and usually not in that order.

During a presentation in a small suburban senior center a woman in her late seventies, who could have been stereotypically cast as a librarian, stood up and told me, "Since I was a little girl I have been passionate about art. I wanted to be an artist, but my father said I should be a secretary, a nurse or a teacher. So I taught English for 34 years. Now that I'm retired I am back into art. On Thursday evenings at 7:30 p.m. I go to 'Naked Body Night' at the Shilough Senior Center. (This is not the center's real name. I don't want to cause a riot there.)

She continued, "A group of us who love to draw hire nude models for the evening class. I'm having the time of my life."

I could see the audience feverishly taking notes about the time and location of Naked Body Night. Be there or be square.

I'll never forget 4'6" Annabelle, who was eager to relate her story to the audience. "I woke up in the hospital one day and didn't know where I was. The nurse informed me, 'Mrs. Baker, you had a heart attack and are in University Hospital. You nearly died.'" And Annabelle said she sat bolt upright in the hospital bed and exclaimed, "I can't die! I need to go home right now. I have a drawer full of sex toys that my grandchildren must not ever find!" The audience roared.

My award for sexiest senior goes to an 84-year-old man named Raymond. Dressed in bib overalls and sporting a

Clark Gable, dyed-jet-black mustache he strolled over confidently after my speech and laid his best lines on me with the Southern drawl of a Georgia gentleman-farmer. "I could tell you were a lady the instant you walked in the room. I like someone with your style. A lot of people these days live together but I'll tell you what, I'm agin it. Would you like to sit with me?"

I said, "Why, Raymond. You're so charming. But I must ask you. Are you a bit of a skirt chaser?" He looked at his shoes and faked embarrassment. "Well, yes, Ma'am, I do have a few lady friends in town." He continued to unabashedly woo me and the only line I think he missed was, "Hey, baby, how about you and me getting out of this place?" It would have been a hard act to pull off since we would've had to bribe the senior center van driver to make our get-away.

I was so impressed with these seniors' joy for life. They embraced disinhibition in the most wonderful sense and we all had a great time.

Let me assure you I am only including the tamer stories. These people were figuratively, and in some cases, literally, living their life "doing the rumba." They beautifully demonstrated that a little disinhibition makes the world go round in a much more delightful fashion.

So I took a cue from these fun-loving people. After months of touring the country from Miami to Seattle, talking to thousands of people 65-101 years of age who'd confessed their passion for dance and sex, I decided to get into the spirit of disinhibition, too.

Even though I had only been taking weekly dance lessons

for a few months I decided to secretly fly my instructor, Manny, to Phoenix where we would perform the foxtrot, salsa and cha cha cha for my next audience. I borrowed a gorgeous long flowing foxtrot gown from my ballroom dancer friend, Louisa, as well as a swishy black skirt and cheetah print knit top for the Latin dances. At our first stop we had 200 enthusiastic retirees straining to see Manny and me twirl about.

I had not danced in front of an audience in almost five decades. Although I had the audacity to do it, I was also pretty inhibited. And the audience could tell. After the performance one woman complimented my dancing, then whispered in my ear, "Next time, honey, put a little wiggle in it."

So for the following performance that day I decided to take her advice. Unbeknownst to Manny I had also borrowed a hot little teal-sequined costume with fringe that was "cut up to there" for the cha cha cha. For my speech I wore a plain black dress with buttons down the front so no one could see what I was secretly wearing underneath. When I concluded my presentation, I turned to the audience and said, "You have inspired me with your passion for life and your willingness to try new things. Now I have a little treat for you."

Manny turned away from me to start the music and at that point I unbuttoned the dress, revealing my costume. The audience oohed and when Manny spun around to see what the audience was responding to his eyes bugged out of his head like a toad catching a fly. The music started just then and I have to tell you I put more than a little wiggle in it. My inhibition center had been drugged to sleep with my adrenaline.

My posture was not perfect, I missed steps, and I was not always on the beat, but I could have lit up Wrigley Field with the smile on my face. To this day I don't know how the audience did what I am about to tell you because they had absolutely no idea we were going to dance. When Manny and I took our bows we looked into the audience and saw 20 of these beautiful seniors each holding up a sign that said, "10"!

Together all of us were living *la vida loca*.

Case in Point: If You Had Three Wishes

Jane Atkinson is a beautiful, professionally accomplished and well-respected woman who decided at the age of 40 that she was living too small and she wanted to change that.

"I was playing it way too safe," she admitted. "So I sat down and had a heart to heart talk with myself. What did I really want?"

The answers came easily.

"I quickly determined I wanted three things," she said. "First, I wanted to be in a loving long-term relationship. Secondly, I wanted to have children in my life. And lastly, I wanted to own a home on the river in my hometown.

"Mary, I love your idea of disinhibition. I have definitely needed to press (and re-press) my disinhibition button at various times in my life. And having set these three intentions I have to tell you my button was about to get a work out!"

One day while walking along the river she thought about her three desires and wondered how to get them. "It took a few weeks but I realized I needed to ask myself a different question, not 'how do I get these?' but 'who do I need to become to have these things in my life?'" she said.

For Jane that meant letting go, as Joseph Campbell wrote, "of the life we have planned, so as to accept the one that is waiting for us."

She saw the barriers in wanting love. "I came to understand that in order to have the long-term relationship I dreamed of I was going to have to be more open to love than I had ever been in my life. I'd never been married and had a pretty strong, effective safety mechanism in place keeping me from letting anyone in. I created a mantra to remind myself, 'I am open to love' and drilled it into my subconscious. I knew that being open to love meant accepting the potential heartache and all the disruption that entails. I needed to let go of being safe and take a risk."

What would a woman open to love do?

While in the throes of a series of "get happy and fabulous" projects, Jane was ready to date and re-posted her online profile. In a matter of weeks Jane met John on-line. They seemed to hit it off at first, but then their correspondence tapered off. Several months later John contacted her again.

Jane explained her response. "Normally, I would not give a guy who had dropped off the radar screen another chance. But I forced myself to have the opposite point of view. I asked myself, 'What would a woman open to love do?'"

John invited her to meet for a glass of wine. "Again, *normally* I was only willing to give an Internet date one hour of my time. But as I drove up I saw him out front, honked and he waved warmly. I thought, 'Oh, this might be okay.'

"We sat down, ordered a drink and then he looked at me and sincerely said, "I can't believe you've never been married. You are gorgeous.'"

John had her attention now and for the next four hours they talked about everything. They met on September 15 and one year to the day later they wed.

All right. Check desire number one off the list.

Bringing children into the picture was a different animal and seemed to require the most disinhibition of all. Jane wasn't entirely clear if she wanted to adopt, bond with step-children or in exactly what configuration the stork might deliver the goods, but she loved kids and knew she wanted a life with them.

Jane said, "However, I had been living comfortably single for a long time and everything was neatly in its place – both physically and emotionally." Her house was contemporary with a white sofa, white shag carpeting, and light hardwood floors, always in perfect condition when company arrived. Kids meant a potentially messy, at times chaotic, unpredictable lifestyle.

"So to have them", Jane admitted, "I had to accept that I was not always going to be in control nor was everything going to be so orderly."

After John and Jane were married, John's 19-year-old daughter got pregnant at college. Jane explains, "I became a step-mom and a grandma all in the same year. We like to joke that my step-daughter had the baby ten years premature."

Her new daughter and grandchild moved in with them for a year. Jane describes her new life: "Messy? Yes. Chaotic? Sometimes. Unpredictable? Absolutely. But oh, what a gift! I would not have changed a minute of it. The reward far outweighed the cost. This new child in the family is the answer to my prayers."

Okay. Cross number two off the list as well.

"So what about the house?" I inquired.

Jane smiled, "When I first thought about buying a home on the river, it was a big stretch financially. My business was doing well and I was in a safe place financially, but I wasn't earning enough to afford the house. To take it up a notch, I asked, 'Who do I need to become to earn my fullest potential?'"

Her answer? An author. She said, "I needed to press that disinhibition button again and be open to outsiders reading my work and possibly criticizing it. That was scary!"

But she met the challenge. It took her just a year to move from blank page to published book. She knew early on that she did not want to sell one book at a time so she developed a system that included a book, a workbook and a three-set CD audio program. She has sold over 6000 copies of her *Wealthy Speaker System*, bringing her a steady stream of new coaching business and a sizable profit. More importantly, she could now afford her dream home.

One day a realtor took the engaged couple to see a property along the river. As the front door opened Jane could see the windows along the back of the house with the river rushing by. She hoped the house had closets because she knew this was home.

In two years Jane completed her list of the three intentions. It is easy to understand why she's a fan of being disinhibited from time to time because she is sure living large now. What it took was a *willingness* to ask new questions and do things she'd never done before. She clearly embraced Reverend Michael Beckwith's advice, "Don't look for your dreams to come true. Look to become true to your dreams."

There is a yin and yang to all of life so I decided to include a second true story here because it illustrates how to use disinhibition in a dramatically different situation from Jane's.

Case in Point #2: Reinventing Yourself

Ann Luckett was a happily married woman with four children. She said, "People would stop us everywhere we went and comment what a beautiful family we were. And I believed it."

Married to Paco, the president of a large international corporation, the family lived a fairy tale life in culturally rich Latin America. They enjoyed a spacious home with a staff of five; interesting, devoted friends; and horses, golf, and tennis.

One night, after making love, lying next to her husband of 30 years, she asked, "Paco, have you ever been unfaithful to me?"

She asked for reasons she still does not understand. She had no suspicions and no plans to question her husband that night.

And the cork flew out of the bottle.

Paco answered, "Ann, I've not been the husband you think I've been."

For the next several hours he admitted to dozens upon dozens of affairs, beginning when she and Paco were dating in college. They got up at three in the morning and made tea in the kitchen. He spewed out countless details, more than she wished she knew. Ann sat in stunned disbelief. By the time the sun came up, a remorseful Paco wished he could put the cork back in the bottle. Life as they'd known it was over.

Ann said, "I went on long walks and cried. I was a mess. I listened to Bonnie Raitt over and over. I had no idea what to do. I'd never considered divorce. In fact, it was the last thing I thought I'd ever do. *My family was my life.*"

She was terrified on many levels, worsened by the fact that she and Paco were going through very difficult financial times. She knew if she left him she'd have little money to take with her. In addition, she had been a devoted corporate wife for nearly three decades. She said, "What kind of a job could I get when my resume read, 'Former yoga teacher and Girl Scout leader?' I was fifty-years-old and needed to start over and reinvent myself. I was about to become my sole economic support. But how on earth would I do that?"

Her grown children were out of college and on their own so Ann had the latitude to make her own decisions. She packed three suitcases and told Paco she wasn't coming back. Now it was his turn to be shocked.

Miserable and clueless as to what to do next, she scraped together enough money to buy a multi-leg airline package and flew back from South America to spend time with family and friends in New York, Colorado, California and Texas. She searched for answers.

She finally settled in El Paso. Her first big test was to learn to live by herself. Ann recalls, "After half a century of life I had never done that before. I went from my parents' home to my sorority house and then to my husband's house at age 21." The loneliness of living by herself soon passed and she discovered she really liked her newfound freedom and the serenity that can come with solitude. But she still needed to make a living and be able to stand on her own. One day a physician friend asked her to be his office manager.

"But I've never done that before," she protested.

He convinced her to take the job and she learned how to run a medical office. A short while later she met a woman at a party who owned an advertising agency and needed a bilingual account executive. Ann resisted again, "But I know nothing about advertising." Her employer-to-be insisted she could teach her. Ann took the job and loved it.

One of her ad accounts was for a motivational speaker who, upon seeing Ann's talent, pleaded, "Come work for me." Of course, Ann pushed back, reasoning that she'd never managed someone's professional career before. It turned out she could.

Then she felt an intense calling to move to Oregon. She packed her green T-top Camaro and, without any job prospects, drove to a state she'd never even visited. Ann recalls, "I had no idea what I was going to do, but intuitively I knew I wanted to go. I decided to be proactive and just show up.

After I arrived I talked to some friends from El Paso who wanted to open a restaurant in Oregon. They literally begged me to run it."

You know the drill by now. Ann had never run a restaurant before, but she was about to.

So far on this odyssey she had purposely chosen cities away from where her adult children lived. She wanted to be completely on her own, separate from her role as wife and mother to figure out who she was. When she had first moved back to the United States she stayed with her children for a while. But she wanted to give them some freedom from her grief as she carved out a new life. She also wanted to protect them from an interruption of their important developmental task of emancipation. She understood that the closer her kids were to her the more responsible they'd feel to put their lives on hold and make sure she was okay.

She, too, needed a comfortable distance to be able to reset the odometer on her life. But now, years later, healed, and with a better a sense of who she was, she longed to be near her family in Colorado Springs. She lived there for eight years, enjoying both managing a boutique full of luscious clothes, rugs and furniture, and getting to know her wonderful grandchildren. She now lives on the garden island of Kauai, after a visit to the island convinced her that was home.

A few weeks after she arrived in Hawaii, Paco died unexpectedly of ruptured duodenal ulcers. She said, "I'll always believe the heavy burden of living a life of lies played a role in his premature death."

In yet another fascinating twist, while going through

Paco's papers, their son, Palo found detailed plans for a new business. He enlisted investors and government interest, and Ann served as Chief of Administration, for this innovative start up renewable energy company. And yes, at first she knew nothing about renewable energy. The refrain, "But I've never done that before" has yet to stop her.

As our conversation wrapped up I asked Ann, "What's the best part of your remarkable journey?"

She smiled, "Being here, talking to you in Kauai, having this story to tell. Living here. Right now. You know," she said, "when I first found out the truth about my marriage I curled up in a chair and cried about my loss for days. I lost the illusion of being married to a man larger than life, and then discovered he was actually the emperor with no clothes. It took me two years to stop walking around saying, 'Oh, God, what happened to my life?' Then one day, in a special ceremony, I blew all my fears, regrets and anger into a balloon and, with the support of a small group of loving friends, I let it go up into the atmosphere. That release was the turning point for me and I could forgive Paco."

Ann continued, "In many ways I know my story sounds like I have evolved at warp speed. But it's all true. I never thought I'd do the things I've described to you. I had to quiet that 'let's be reasonable' part of my psyche and ignore the voice that warned, 'You can't do that. It's not like you.' I now know it's better if I don't try to force the outcomes, because when I stopped trying to control them, they've been beyond my wildest imagination. I love my life today more than I ever have."

Lessons for Us All: The Power of Telling a New Story

I so admire these two smart, strong women. At first glance you might think that a 40-year-old, financially-stable, childless, unmarried woman and a 50-year-old, broke, divorced mother of four would have little in common. But in many ways they are so much alike. They asked themselves what they wanted and set an intention to change their lives for the better. They were gutsy and did things they'd never done before, over and over again until they got what they wanted. They proved that reinvention is possible despite what looks like long, nearly impossible odds. They believed in themselves and in the infinite possibilities that lay ahead of them. They were *willing*. But first, they had to become *disinhibited*.

We grow to the degree that we are willing to transcend our story.

My good friend, Kris Westphal, invited her five-year-old twin nieces over to her house for an arts and crafts day. Catie and Claire diligently went to work with crayons and paper to each write a story. Catie proudly handed Kris her creation, featuring a colorful flower with an entire page of scribbles. Kris admired the artwork and then inquired, "Tell me your story. What does your writing say?"

Catie looked up at Kris and replied matter-of-factly, "I don't know. I can't read."

Her sister, Claire, still busily composing, asked, "How do you spell 'ponna'?"

Kris replied, "Well, gee, I don't think ponna is a word."

"Aunt Kris," Claire chided, "Yes, *it is!* Come on! 'Once a ponna time...'"

The pure innocence of these two five-year-olds writing their stories made me stop to think about one of the best pieces of wisdom I ever received:

We grow to the degree that we are willing to transcend our story.

We each know our story *so* well: The tale we love to tell about how we can't save consistently because we've just never been good with money; the drama-filled saga about how we struggle with relationships because of our childhood issues; the fascinating accounts of how we can't lose weight, go on vacation, get a better job, return to college, or find any time for ourselves because blah, blah, blah...

We repeat the story line over and over, with detailed accounts from the past that prove our limitations. Our old stories are often full of blame, shame and insecurities, not to mention slightly exaggerated "facts." We repeat the stories to ourselves so often we internalize them and believe every word, making them our truth.

Jane and Ann are beautiful examples of two women who succeeded by being willing to transcend their story. They each could have kept telling the same sad tale, how there are no good men out there, and money is hard to come by, and they're too old to reinvent their careers and so on and so on. They could have remained convinced of their limitations and continued to convince others about the "truth" of their lives as well. I believe the key to living the life of their dreams stemmed from telling a new story--one chock full of disinhibition. Like Catie and Claire they set their inhibitions aside and wrote new stories, even though they did not yet know how to "read" or "spell."

I, too, want to write new stories about my life. So when I catch myself launching into the familiar rendition, I stop and preface the opening sentence with the phrase, *"Up until now..."*

I spent the last year focusing on this simple strategy.

My old story: I am just not good with computers.

This is one of my favorite stories and I tell it often. *Up until now*, in a word association game, if someone said, "Windows" I would say, "drapes." If they said, "Attachment," I would reply, "Disorder." An Apple was something that kept the doctor away. Social media was inviting friends over for pizza and a movie. Tweets were for birds and whistles.

I decided to transcend that story.

My new story: I am the face of techno-mastery. I enjoy learning the ins and outs of linking in and logging on to connect with friends and colleagues all over the world. I am devoted to my weekly computer lessons with the One to One program at the Apple store. For just $99 I get 52, weekly, individual, face-to-face lessons on any techno-gadgets that start with an "i". That's $1.92 an hour. I get

> As soon as one old story line starts to fall away many of the other countless subplots begin to lose their power as well.

more proficient each week and I am starting to make these computers sing.

Like my dancing I am still technically a rookie, but according to my new story I have mastered the skills I need to make my computers my near and dear friends. That's my story and I am sticking to it.

As you might suspect, as soon as one old story line starts to fall away many of the other countless subplots begin to lose their power as well. Just as in Jane and Ann's lives, when they transcended the first part of their story they watched in gratitude and glee as a long line of other dominos fell in rapid succession. They both agree if they had clung to their former versions they would not have been able to take the next steps into wonderful new lives.

So, I invite you, for the next week, to catch yourself telling "your story" and rephrase it beginning with "*Up until now.*" And then write your new story...

"Once a ponna time..."

Let's Get Ready to Rumba

Are you willing to get disinhibited and try things you've never done before? Can you hush up your frontal lobe long enough to start your own Naked Body Night? Does it sound like fun to fill your drawer with sexy things like Annabelle did? Maybe you'll actually wear those purple fuzzy slippers to the office. How willing are you to transcend your old story? What does your new story sound like? The answers to these questions will help you take your next step.

Accepting the Invitation

Dear Mary,

The story below was something I observed at a meeting a couple of years ago. I remembered it during a dream last week and I thought of you.

Ms. Meeting Planner gazed at her attendees and sighed. They were all glued to their seats around the perimeter of the deserted parquet wood dance floor. It was the pre-conference reception and even though Gloria Estefan charged them to "Get on Your Feet" and the DJ tried to entice, cajole, and bribe the group to get up and dance—they weren't budging.

In sheer desperation, Ms. Meeting Planner went around the room, leaned over and pleaded with the attendees one-by-one to please help get the party started—let loose—have a little fun. Just get up and dance! One by one I could see them shake their heads from side to side, smile wanly and tell her, "I can't dance."

I marveled at how self-conscious the group, primarily women, seemed to be. Where was their enthusiasm, their sense of fun, their joie de vivre?

Ms. Meeting Planner was completing her trek around the floor, imploring folks all along the way to "just give it a try," when she came to a participant who was there with her five-year-old granddaughter. The woman was attempting to explain, like all the others, that she couldn't dance. And then her granddaughter looked up, smiled at Ms. Meeting Planner and announced, "I can dance!" Before anyone could say another word, the little girl skipped out onto the dance floor and began hopping and jumping to the beat, giggling and having the time of her life.

And then the grandmother got up to join her. While they both laughed and had a good time, another attendee rose and joined them. And then another. And another. And another—until the dance floor was almost jammed with people bopping to the music and having a great time.

What enabled that young girl to do what all the adults could not—or would not? She had something that the other people in the room had lost—confi-dance! She wasn't thinking to herself, "What if Susan thinks I look silly?" or "What if Jim thinks I'm an idiot?" or "What if I make a fool of myself?" She was willing to express her belief in herself and in her abilities by getting up and DANCING!

How many opportunities for joy, fun, and happiness we miss because we're concerned what other people might think. Go ahead, get on your feet. Dance like nobody's watching. Embrace your confi-dance!

Fondly,

Karyn

THE LESSON: *GET DISINHIBITED*

Be willing to do something you've never done before.
Say, "Up until now."
Tell a new story the way you want it to be.
Put a little wiggle in it.

Take Your Next Step

What is your new story?

Chapter Five

Surrender

The quickest way to access all of your true potential and actually experience it is the power of surrender.

--Greg Barrette

After just a few dance lessons I felt, acted, and walked differently. I stood in line at the grocery store poised as if I was just about to take off fox-trotting, which embarrassed my children so much they waited in the car. I waltzed my luggage through the airport. I'd absent-mindedly do some little cha-cha-cha moves coming out of church. My friends, terribly amused, wanted to know what was going on. I'd motion them closer and confide, "I'm taking dance lessons." Then I'd beam.

One good friend, wondering aloud how a few dance lessons could make me so radiant, commented, "Well, as a single woman it must be a great way to get out and about."

I smiled at him. "I fly over 100,000 miles a year for work. I'm pretty much out and about already."

"Well, then, I bet it's just nice to have a man hold you in his arms," he offered.

I looked down my nose at him. "C'mon, we're not groping in a nightclub at 2 a.m. It's a ballroom dance lesson."

"Okay, then. I give up. What is it?" he asked.

I knew exactly what it was. I leaned toward my friend and murmured in his ear, "*He leads.*"

My friend looked at me in disbelief, "What do you mean, '*He leads?*'"

"For the entire hour my instructor directs my every move. My main job is to follow," I explained.

My friend laughed out loud. "You, Little Ms. Independence, the take-charge feminist who heads a successful business, raised three children, serves as a spokesperson for a number of causes and products-- just to name a few of your leadership roles—YOU want to be LED?

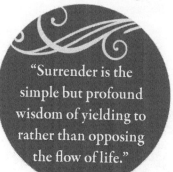

"Surrender is the simple but profound wisdom of yielding to rather than opposing the flow of life."

"Yes. Yes, I do," I replied confidently.

Oh, I know. Believe me, I know. Surrender is the last thing most of us want to do. Keep in mind, I did not say "submit." The concepts of surrender and submit are as different as Emily Post and Snookie.

To get a handle on what surrender really is I consulted the works of the go-to-guy of surrender, spiritual teacher Eckert Tolle. "To some people," he writes, "surrender may have negative connotations, implying defeat, giving up, failing to rise to the challenges of life, becoming lethargic, and so on. True surrender, however is something entirely different. It does not mean to passively put up with whatever situation you find yourself in and to do nothing about it. Nor does it mean to cease making plans or initiating positive action. Surrender is the simple but profound wisdom of yielding to rather than opposing the flow of life."

Surrendering to the flow of life--that was exactly what I felt. I came to understand that dance is actually a series of invitations to surrender.

Let's say the leader wants the follower to turn. A good leader invites the follower to do that by simply holding her hand gently and then raising his arm straight up just slightly higher than her head. He does not actively turn his partner. He compresses her hand ever so slightly in the direction he wants her to go. There is no pulling or pushing. His actions merely say, "I would like you to turn now." The move requires a yes, a surrender, as she agrees to step into the space he has created for her by lifting his arm.

No one gets to dance unless the follower is willing to surrender. She does not cede her power, not for one instant. Actually, upon her decision to be led, all the power shifts to her. He can invite all day but until she says, "I accept," nothing happens. He opens the door. She and only she is in charge of walking through it, making the dance possible.

Why does she walk through it? Many reasons, but the first one is key: She surrenders because in doing so she lets the leader do *his job*. The leader is in charge of four things:

1. Rhythm changes
2. Direction: left, right, back or forward
3. Dance position: Open, closed, promenade
   (and you're going to love this next one)
4. *Making his partner look really good.*

Who knew? His every move, gesture, posture- it's all designed to make the follower the star. And people wonder why I like to dance.

The follower's job is to surrender her resistance to letting someone make her feel beautiful, graceful, radiant, talented, competent, and strong. She taps into the power of surrender and *voila*, the Goddess in her emerges.

Everyone also needs a rhythm of renewal.

But isn't it better to lead, you ask? We read books and go to conferences to develop our leadership skills. No one studies how to be a better follower. Well, they should. From a life balance point of view it is impossible to *always* be the leader. While it's true everyone leads something--a workplace, a family, the free world, --it is equally true that *everyone also needs a rhythm of renewal.*

If you lead all the time you will burn out and become unable to lead. We must, men and women alike, ask ourselves, "To what or whom will I surrender?" It might be to eight hours of sleep. We know we'll feel more powerful in the morning. Perhaps we surrender to our God or life partner or faithful dog, who simply will not take no for an answer when he wants you to throw the ball. We are both leaders *and* followers. It's a duality that exists in all of nature: light/

dark, yin/yang, hot/cold, and male/female. Our ability to surrender allows us to fill back up, and renew ourselves so we can lead our tribe once again.

Surrender is where all the power lies.

Still, so many of us refuse to lay down our arms, surrender to the flow of life

"Without faith, we're frantically trying to control what is not our business to control, and fix what it is not in our power to fix."

and let someone else (or Someone Else) stand guard for a while. We do not let them make us look or feel good. We might be exhausted, angry, terrified or worse, but dammit, at least we are in charge, leading even when we feel powerless.

While we usually use surrender as a verb in this context, in reality, it is more than something we do. It's an attitude we adopt, a way of viewing the world. It's the sense of relief we feel as our resistance drops and good rushes in. It's tapping into the infinite potential, and listening to the sound of all those quarks collapse on our behalf.

Yes, surrender requires faith and trust. Marianne Williamson, author of A Return to Love, wrote, "To trust in a force that moves the Universe is faith. Faith isn't blind, it's visionary. Faith is believing that the Universe is on our side, and that the Universe knows what It's doing. Faith is a psychological awareness of an unfolding force for good, constantly at work in all dimensions. Our attempts to direct this force only interfere with it. Our willingness to relax into it allows it to work on our behalf. Without faith, we're frantically trying to control what is not our business to control, and fix what it is not in our power to fix. What we're trying to fix can't be fixed by us anyway. Without faith, we're wasting time."

When the follower fails to wait for the lead and instead initiates the dance move we call it back leading. One day, when I was having a hard time trusting and I might have even been trying to lead just a teeny tiny bit, Manny stopped me and said, "You need to know, Mary, *nobody likes a back leader.*" I knew he was right. I think I try to lead in an attempt to anticipate what move is next, so I can do it correctly, and this relieves my anxiety. I needed to learn to trust that the lead would come, followed by the inevitability of a choice: to follow or not. I was trying to do well what I had no business doing in the first place.

Yielding to Win

As foreign as it may sound we actually have a lot of experience with the power of surrender. For example, several of the martial arts, such as tai chi, aikido, and judo, advocate the power of yielding to win. They use the flow of their opponent's energy to their advantage. In sports we also learn to yield to win. A bunt or a sacrifice fly advances a player for the good of the baseball team. Spiking the football or throwing it out of bounds stops the clock. Punting the ball downfield is a form of surrender to gain a safer field position. In the game of chess we may let our opponent capture our castle to get our knight into a checkmate position three moves later. Losing the battle to win the war is a time-tested strategy.

Case in Point: Surrendering One Day at a Time

Chad Hymas is an expert in the power of surrender. On April 3, 2001 Chad was preparing to feed the cattle on his ranch in rural Utah. He was using a tractor with a lift to remove a 2000-pound bale of hay out of the loft. The hydraulic lift malfunctioned and the bale fell two stories, crushing Chad and breaking his neck. Forty-five minutes later his wife, Shondell, found him trapped under the bale with his face pinned to the steering wheel of the tractor. Chad was unable to move and she could not tell if he was even alive. Frantically she called the volunteer fire department and miraculously, in a matter of fifteen minutes, eight cowboys arrived and superhumanly lifted the equivalent of a pickup truck off of her husband.

Unbelievable as it was that he survived, the accident tragically left Chad a quadriplegic. He is quick to point out, however, that his dreams were not paralyzed that day. So let me tell you the happy ending up front.

Since that fateful event Chad has become a Hall of Fame professional speaker, motivating people to "use their wings and reach seemingly impossible heights." The *Wall Street Journal* called him one of the ten most inspirational people in the world. He has maintained his hobby and dream of managing a 5100-acre elk preserve with his father. He races in marathons and set a world record by wheeling his chair from Salt Lake City to Las Vegas (513 miles in 11 days). His proudest accomplishment is the relationship he has with his family. He's married to his high school sweetheart and the love of his life, Shondell. They are the proud parents of four children. He has exceeded his (and everyone else's) wildest imaginations.

Chad's remarkable story ironically begins before he was injured. Just three months prior to his accident, Chad's father, Kelly, an insurance agent and broker, attended his company's convention in Dallas where Art Berg, a quadriplegic, was the dynamic keynote speaker. Kelly was so impressed with Art and his philosophy of life that he bought Art's DVD. When Kelly got home he enthusiastically invited his sons and daughters-in-law to his home to watch it. But, schedules being what they are, everyone was too busy and the family night of DVD viewing never happened.

After the accident Kelly brought the DVD to the hospital and he and Chad watched it together. The next day, without telling his son, Kelly called Art's office and told his assistant about the accident.

Chad relates what happened ten days later.

"A man in a wheelchair rolls into my hospital room. He does not introduce himself. In fact, he doesn't say a word. He wheels toward me and transfers himself into my bed. Lying next to me he proceeds to take off *all* his clothes and then he puts them all back on. He gets back into his wheel chair, spins around to face me and says, 'Hi. I'm Art Berg.'

"Art has a broken neck at the same spinal level as I do. He knew exactly what I desperately needed to know. He was prepared to show me how to be independent and live a great life, not in spite of, but perhaps even because of my fate. We talked for about ten minutes.

"And for the next nine months I surrendered the lead to him. Actually, I have to confess, I kind of stalked him, even following him to Hawaii to hear him speak at the National Speakers Association's winter conference. I didn't want to be a speaker at the time. I just wanted Art to teach me, by example, how to be a good husband and father. We went to the Pro Bowl in Honolulu and had a great time together.

"Two days later Art died suddenly from an infection. I was devastated. I can't be more emphatic when I say the guy transformed my life and, in gratitude, I use his lessons every day."

In the beginning, however, Chad regretfully says he was not willing to surrender to much. "Initially, I resisted everything." He admits to times of bitterness, shocked at the loss of what seemed like--well --everything. He'd owned a landscape construction company with 35 employees and had dreams of running an elk ranch. "I was in despair. How could my life have taken such an incredibly sudden turn for the worse?"

He continued, "You have to know that what I can't stand the most is pity. Shondell and I had been married for seven years. I didn't want her to have to deal with me paralyzed in a wheelchair. I loved her too much to be a burden so I told her to take the two kids and start a new life without me. She flatly refused to consider my request. I was in the hospital for 63 days and she was there every day for me.

"When I came home things got worse. I was fighting to get my clothes on. It was embarrassing to have my wife watch me fail. One day while Shondell showered me, I got angry, yelled at her and kicked her out of the room. My mother-in-law intuitively called about that time and she asked to talk to me. She was very caring but direct when she said, 'Shondell loves you. The greatest thing about marriage is not sex. The greatest thing is gracious acceptance. Be willing to be grateful for the things you were not previously grateful for.'

"Shondell came back in the room. I cried and apologized. She said, 'You lost your body. But we still have everything that means the most to us: the boys, our health, our home, faith, hope and our love for each other. '

"In that moment I learned who Shondell really is. She taught me how to surrender and become more powerful in the process. I got quite a lesson that day: Whatever your loss is, use gracious acceptance."

One day Shondell gave him the book, *Men Are From Mars, Women Are From Venus*. Chad laughs, "When I finished it I thought, 'That is the stupidest book I've ever read.'"

This was not the response Shondell was hoping for. Chad admits he failed to hear and respond to his wife's clear message that they'd been through a lot and she now wanted to re-focus on their relationship. Chad confessed, "As a result our marriage went downhill. So..."he sighed, "I read the book again and when I surrendered to the new ideas about the differences between men and women and how Shondell and I could better meet each other's needs, our marriage improved tenfold. I realized that I had to let go of my old attitudes, and open up to new ideas."

Still, Chad recalled, pockets of resistance remained. "Five years after my accident I still had not gone hunting, which had been one of my greatest joys since I was a young boy walking through the woods alongside my dad. Each year my father would coax me to join him but again, my pride told me I would just be a burden.

"My dad would not let up. 'Don't you still love campfires, the timber and tents?'

I replied, 'Of course I still love them, but I just can't do that anymore.'

My father finally relented but added, 'Okay then, but I want you to know I'm taking your boys without you. You're robbing them of a great appreciation for the outdoors.'"

Chad continued, "I didn't like it one bit that he was taking my sons without me. Once the boys were in the picture I surrendered immediately. I went hunting and I haven't missed a season since. You know, my boys grew up with a dad who doesn't walk. It is not a problem for them. The idea that it is a problem belongs solely to me."

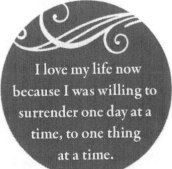

I love my life now because I was willing to surrender one day at a time, to one thing at a time.

Chad paused and then said, "So you are right, Mary. I love my life now because I was willing to surrender one day at a time, to one thing at a time. I can now see how surrender was the key to my success. I wish it had not taken so long to learn this lesson, but perhaps it all came in divine order. We can only take that step in our own time."

I know this is the part of the chapter where I am supposed to summarize his message but I think Chad said it all beautifully so I will just say, gratefully, *Amen*.

Trust

The dynamic duo of trust and surrender is like the chicken and the egg dilemma. No one can say which one comes first but everyone agrees a new way of life requires both. As I wrote this book I researched everything I could about surrender, probably because it is what I resist and most need to learn. But I considered myself pretty well versed in trust. Apparently, the Universe did not agree and one day, while I was working on this book, it sent me a reminder about what trust looks like.

If a writer is lucky "the muse shows up" and dictates the words to you. All you have to do is listen and type as fast as you can. An author receives this gift with a mix of gratitude, awe, and ecstasy. It is a not-to-be-missed event because you never know when the muse will start talking so you have to be ready to capture the download. You also fear you'll have no idea how to re-establish communication if the Orator, much to your dismay, suddenly falls silent.

It was in this spirit that, on my third day of a new yoga class in Hawaii, I put a pad of paper and a pen in front of my mat. The muse had been sending me some very creative lines during the last two classes, and I had serious monkey-mind trying to remember what came over the bamboo wireless. My yoga instructor, Eagle, walked up to me gently and smiled, his eyes twinkling in amusement. "What's that?" he asked, pointing to my little makeshift desk.

"Well, when I practice yoga I get such great ideas for this book I'm currently writing that I want to just jot them down so I don't forget," I stammered.

Eagle has a calm, confident, and radiant aura about him and he smiled again. If this had been boot camp he would have shouted, "What kind of idiot are you? You cannot 'practice' yoga, concentrating on the sound of your breath and write a book at the same time! Give me 50 push-ups!"

No, instead he spoke from his inner Buddha and said, "Mary, you must trust that the words will come to you. There is a collective field where all those ideas reside and you can access that field at any time." Then he told me the story of Sri Ramana Marharshi, the Indian sage who, at the age of 16, ran away from home and went to Arunachala Mountain, referred to as the spiritual heart of the world. For weeks the young man walked slowly "like a woman in the last month of pregnancy," around and around the nine-mile mountainous circuit. In this deep meditation he connected to the collective field to which Eagle had alluded. With access to all information, Sri Ramana knew, without any previous exposure, the sacred Vedas verbatim. This is a miracle the equivalent of walking through the Mall of America and completely understanding organic chemistry by the time you get to Bed Bath and Beyond.

"All knowledge," Eagle instructed me, "is available to us if we stay conscious."

Recognizing the ridiculous yoga faux pas I had just committed, I sheepishly put away my paper and pen and refocused on the sounds of my inhalations and exhalations.

Later that day I went to the Princeville library in Kauai to get a new card. While waiting in line I plucked a book off a nearby shelf *at random* called *Born to Be Good: The Science of a Meaningful Life* by Dacher Keltner. I swear to you, without looking, I opened the book to page 219 and there was the heading entitled: *Trust.*

Reading within this section, I found these words:

"Dance is the most reliable and quickest route to a mysterious feeling that has gone by many names over the generations: sympathy, agape, ecstasy, jen; here I'll call it trust. **To dance is to trust.**"

That day I learned that the information I needed to write this book was not only in the collective consciousness field. Apparently at least some of it was also in the Princeville library on a little dot of land called Kauai, there just for the asking, *if only I would trust.*

We have to trust that we will find what we need at the time that we need it.

Daily headlines remind us how often our trust has been breached in the last few years. It would not be difficult to build a case, therefore, that we should stop trusting, period. Actually, I think the opposite is true. We need to trust more than ever. We have to trust that we will find what we need at the time that we need it. We have to trust that we are not alone. We have to trust that the next lead will come and we will know what to do and the dance will continue.

It starts with being trustworthy ourselves and constantly looking for the good. Despite the reports, trust abounds.

A postscript to this whole story: I shared the details with my Internet readership and got the following reply from Wendy Treynor, who coincidentally had just signed up for my next retreat: "Dacher Keltner was my mentor in graduate school and wrote my letter of recommendation for my Ph.D. program at the University of Michigan."

And guess what she wrote her dissertation paper on.

Trust.

I often wonder in these situations if this is the Universe just showing off, like the dolphins who trail cruise ships, leaping out the water and doing spins, putting on an impromptu Sea World exhibition in the wild. Or maybe the quarks are feeling frisky in their subatomic world, drinking margaritas and doing the limbo (or even the international rumba), bragging to the other particles, "Hey, watch *this*!" I have to believe these events, woven across time and distance, are interrelated and of great consequence. I paid lots of attention to this lesson on trust.

Holy Surrender, Wholly Surrender

I hope none of us will ever deal with the enormity of surrender that Chad faced after his accident. Still, we will have ample opportunity to explore and use this concept in our own lives as we prepare to move forward.

No matter the exact details, we all have to face the surrender to "what is," the unvarnished reality of our lives. That means accepting that our past is over and unchangeable. We cannot undo the heartbreak or recreate the missed opportunities. Some windows have closed. This time around I will not be a NASA engineer, the biological mother of any more children or a Brazilian supermodel. I surrender to those truths.

I had an email discussion with my brother, Bill Schulte, about this concept of the "closed window theory" and surrender.

He replied:

I have been thinking about what you wrote. I agree with the value of surrender. You may recall in the movie Star Wars, *Obi Wan Kenobi surrenders to Darth Vader and Luke surrenders to the Force, which led to the greater good. I also agree that graciously accepting who you are, warts and all, is important. But I find it hard to know how surrender applies to everyday situations. Where does accepting end and giving up begin? Your examples are good, but if you wanted to be a NASA engineer and can't be, do you transmute that desire into becoming a space buff instead? Do you take your biological maternal yearnings and decide to adopt or work at a childcare agency? Exactly what do you do with your Brazilian supermodel dreams?*

Maybe in everyday life, surrender works more like this: When I coached Little League and parents railed at me about something, I never got mad or argued with them. I always told them, "Isn't Little League great? No matter what happens, good or bad, it gives you a terrific opportunity to talk with your kid about it. What could be better than that?"

Am I asking them to surrender to the situation? Rather than fight for what they "want," don't these parents gain something much more valuable if they take the opportunity to teach their children important lessons? An opportunity which is lost by resisting?

I wonder if we can find the answers to the insightful

questions Bill poses in the "free will clause" humans bring with them. Free will is everyone's birthright. We get to decide how surrender plays out in our lives. Remember, surrender does not mean passivity. We stay engaged, make plans and initiate positive actions. For example, I might be so happy dancing that I forget all about my windows of opportunity that have closed. On the other hand, who knows? Maybe I will adopt a Brazilian supermodel and send her to aeronautical engineering school. Hey, it could happen.

I believe we are often much more proficient at surrendering to what is than we give ourselves credit for. We surrender to what is when we accept that, despite our wish that it was different, in this lifetime we are going to remain a certain gender, race, height, sexual orientation or eye color. We surrender to what is when we balance our checkbook and acknowledge a serious shortfall. We practice the art of surrender as we sit patiently in a traffic jam knowing we'll miss our child's soccer game or the long-ago scheduled meeting with the big client. Surrender allows us to calmly wait until our two-year-old son or thirteen-year-old daughter finishes the temper tantrum. *We surrender to what is when we lean into what is.*

We have to see the X on the map that says, "You are *here*." X marks the spot where we begin to let go of the past, stop worrying about the future and focus on what's happening now. X is the place where we explore the inequities caused by being the "wrong" sex, color or size. We stand on the X and

We surrender to what is when we lean into what is.

make a plan about how to parent more effectively, increase our cash flow or reconnect with our important business prospects.

Just as refusing to surrender to our partner stops the dance, refusing to surrender to life creates an inner resistance to the is-ness of our reality--*which stops our forward motion like nothing else can.* But, if we can learn to surrender we'll no longer have to cling to the illusion of control. If we can trust enough to let go and receive guidance, we can allow someone else to be a force for our good. We can say to ourselves, "Ahhhhh. What a relief! I don't have to do everything, pick up on every signal, sort it all out and make sense of it." We can surrender wholly--without hesitation, without worry, without regret--as a holy act. Then we can move forward and ease into the flow of life.

Accepting the Invitation

Dear Mary,

It was very nice to talk with you about how I had to find my power in surrender. As Chad's wife, I never questioned whether I would stay with him. I always knew I loved him. The therapists at the hospital did counsel us, however, that couples in our situation often get divorced, either because the quadriplegic pushes away or the uninjured spouse cannot adjust. I knew Chad would have to push awfully hard to get me to leave.

Everyone always asks me, "How did you do it?"

The answer is: I surrendered.

My first surrender came when Chad was still in the hospital. I would get up very early every day, find someone to watch our little boys, drive an hour and a half to the hospital, spend eight to ten hours with Chad, drive home, pick up the kids, and after I got them to bed, I'd return calls to all the people who wanted updates.

At night I felt very alone but it gave me time to really think. That is when I made the decision to surrender. In my mind, adjusting to the situation was my only option. Some people might argue that I had other choices. But I knew I wanted Chad. I knew the desired end result and it was clear to me that if I was going to get what I wanted most-- which was him--then I'd have to willingly and gratefully take on this challenge.

Yes, of course there were dark days. In the hospital we had lots of support, and surrounded by patients like him, Chad was positive and upbeat. But when we got home we were back in our old life and Chad couldn't do what he used to do: work or coach basketball or ranch. I couldn't do what I used to do either. We had three-year-old and one year old sons. Each morning I'd get up, feed the kids, get Chad ready (which took hours), and fix lunch. Then I'd help Chad with his physical therapy, (he had to do it at home since the hospital was so far away) do the laundry, make dinner, and spend hours putting everyone to bed. There was no time for me.

I'd crawl into bed thinking, "Tomorrow will be just the same. There's got to be more to my life than just surviving." Because that was precisely what I was doing, just surviving to get to the next day. And that's when the second surrender happened. I am a very spiritual person. I realized that I'd been given a great gift. I was to serve. Some people have to look for ways to serve. I did not have to find a way.

With a better attitude and a perspective on the big picture, life got better. We figured things out, and got into a routine. We went back to enjoying the journey.

Life is "normal" again. We are busy! Our family has even expanded. Even though I tried to convince myself that I was fine with two beautiful little boys, I knew something was missing. I had always wanted a daughter. So we adopted four-month-old Gracie. When Chad gives his speeches he often says to his high school students in the audience, "I am now going to tell you where babies come from. They come from Guatemala."

We are also parents to our newest son, ten-year-old Jordan. The State of Utah removed him from a difficult home situation and we are thrilled he is now part of our family. Though he lags a bit academically, he's very bright and is excelling at school for the first time. He also had three surgeries this summer to repair his cleft lip and palate and he got braces. He said the other day, "Mom, I just can't stop smiling." You can imagine how that makes both Chad and me feel.

Before the accident we were a very happy family. I used to say our theme song was, "Just Another Day in Paradise." We still feel that way. Chad and I are closer after all we have been through and as much in love as ever.

You asked me what was the biggest advantage to surrendering? Feeling grateful. When I was sixteen and dreaming of the future, my picture perfect life looked like this: Married to a man that I loved and who loved me, great kids, all of us happily living on a ranch, financially stable, actively involved in our community and at church. While I was devastated by

Chad's accident, over time, I realized I still had everything I dreamed of. I am glad Chad and I both surrendered. We share a wonderful life!
Sincerely,
Shondell Hymas

THE LESSON: *SURRENDER*

Yield to win.
Don't do well what you have no business doing.
Trust: Have faith in an unfolding force for good.
Use surrender to adopt a rhythm of renewal.

Take Your Next Step

To what or whom do you resist surrendering?

—◦◦✧◦◦—

Chapter Six

Keep Doing Your Basic Steps

—◦◦✧◦◦—

The map of abundance and joy has always existed. It has always been about the basics. Sometimes we just forget what the basics are.

--Earnie Larsen

I had set my intention to dance and was putting three to six hours a week into lessons and practice. I'd quit many of my irritating little habits, although I still ducked once in a while. I had embraced ambiguity by going to each lesson, okay with the fact that I still pretty much had no idea what I was doing. I even surrendered the lead (most of the time). My new focus was learning the actual dance steps.

Each dance has a basic pattern. For example, the country two-step is quick, quick, slow, slow, moving counterclockwise around the floor. The foxtrot pattern is slow, slow, quick, quick, often done in a box formation. And the salsa, as they say in Miami is, *uno, dos, tres,* HOLD, *quatro, cinco, seis.*

These are the basic steps. Anyone watching can see what dance you are performing by the steps you're taking. If you're not doing the basic step of one, two, three, one, two, three, with a rise and fall motion, you are not doing the waltz.

One day Manny led me through some elaborate cha-cha-cha moves, turning and twisting me in ways he'd never done before. Frustrated, I got lost and stopped.

He said, "Mary, you do not have to know what move is coming next. All you have to do is keep executing your basic steps: two, and three, cha cha cha, four and one, cha cha cha. No matter what *I* do, *you* just keep your feet moving and do the basic steps. *Don't stop.*"

Since it seems that it takes a village to teach me to dance, I had an ironically identical experience with my other instructor. Taylor explained, "When the leader invites you to dance he expects two things. First, that you will surrender the lead to him. And second, that no matter what he does, you will keep doing the basic step - over and over- until he stops leading."

Some Basic Advice on Basic Steps: *Don't Stop*

The message was clear. If I wanted to take the next step, to learn new dances and become better at this art form I'd have to keep doing my basics. I also knew I had just been tutored in a life lesson. Under stress, many of us stop doing our basic steps, and just like I did in my dance lesson, we get lost.

We disconnect from the underlying structure that keeps us in balance.

In a weird irony only humans could create, we stop doing what we know will support us as we move forward. We give up exercising and eating well. We close our books and anesthetize ourselves by channel surfing. We cut back on sleep, scrap our plans with friends, skip breakfast, cancel our dentist appointments or forget to call home as often as we did before. We yell at our kids, our partners, and the poor girl behind the counter. We stop laughing. We forget our manners. We disconnect from the underlying structure that keeps us in balance.

Like the inventor of the hammer to whom everything looks like a nail, for the next few months I saw basics in every situation. I couldn't read a novel, attend a concert or wash my hair without seeing "BASICS" flashing in neon. Convinced of their value I attempted to systematically unravel the mystery of basics, particularly as they apply to issues in everyday life, including physical, financial and spiritual well-being.

First, I found an article in *USA Today* about the growing girth of Americans. Donna Ryan, the president of the Obesity Society, a group of weight loss researchers and professionals, was quoted saying that there are four critical basics to successful weight loss:

First, create a caloric deficit. I flashed back to my many attempts at weight loss. There were some doozies. I tried the Russian Air Force diet. I was sure it was the answer. Have you ever seen an obese Russian military pilot? Then there were the Cabbage, Grapefruit, and Banana diets. At least they were cheap. I even went on the Five Day Caveman diet. Okay. I have no idea about the rationale there. The point is, whether it's Weight Watchers, Atkins or the All You Can Eat Kumquat diet, it can't work without a caloric deficit.

The next basic is to monitor food intake. Our minds, tricky little devils that they are, lull us into thinking "I eat like a bird," but fail to disclose the detail that the avian we are referring to is Big Bird. We must be willing to out ourselves and write down everything we ingest. Research shows that keeping a food diary really works. When we stop losing weight it's often because we are no longer keeping these records and, without noticing, we start feeding Big Bird again.

The third basic is to track exercise expenditures. Right away I saw a big problem with this advice because only 17 percent of people report that they exercise while on a weight loss diet. I also knew from behavioral research that some people exaggerate ever so slightly when reporting good habits, not that I am implying any of us would. But the importance of exercise cannot be overstated if we want to continue to fit into just one airline seat. In fact, according to the National Weight Loss Registry at the University of Colorado School of Medicine, people who lose weight and keep it off for a year or more exercise *an average for 60 to 90 minutes every day*.

Lastly, Ryan advised, "Weigh yourself regularly." For many of us this is as much fun as trying on bathing suits under florescent lights. According to a Consumer Reports Health Survey, 60% of us rarely or never weigh ourselves. But in this case, ignorance is apparently not bliss. We have to mix our trite metaphors and face the music, swallow the toad, step up to the plate, and get on the damn scale so we get accurate feedback and adjust our weight loss efforts accordingly.

Ryan said, "If you adhere to the basics, chances are you'll

succeed." What she was too polite to say is that if you fail to adhere to her advice your odds of success go down and your pant size goes up.

When I finished the article I wasn't sure if I was discouraged or reassured. On one hand losing weight seemed nearly impossible, and on the other hand, there they were, just four basics that, when adhered to, held out the promise that I might avoid the dress department at Tent City. More importantly, the list meant I would know what I needed to do when I complained, "I just can't seem to lose the weight."

Let me be clear about something here. Being overweight is one of the most complicated medical conditions there is and some people have a much more difficult time with it than others for reasons scientists do not yet completely understand. But for most of us, the problem is more related to over-active forks and under-active gym shoes than it is to sluggish glands.

In *USA Today*, I also found important investment basics. I read a discussion about how to avoid putting money into a Ponzi scheme, which unfortunately for many recent investors could have been titled, "How to Close the Barn Door After the Horse Is Out." Nevertheless, the authors made the basics for safe investing quite clear. First, the experts warned, if you don't understand it, don't buy it, and secondly, if it sounds

Forgive your enemies, even *that* enemy--*especially* that one.

waaaaaay too good to be true, it probably is. A consistent high rate of return in down markets is not just a red flag. It's like the 300,000 movie extras in the film *Gandhi* screaming simultaneously, "Don't do it!" Failure to follow these simple basic steps of investing could cost you your life savings.

Finally, I didn't need to be a religious scholar to learn in a quick review of the literature that the spiritual community, from the Sufi poets to the Southern Baptists, agree on some pretty consistent basics: Get still every day and connect to your Source; forgive your enemies (yes, they all insist **you** forgive all your enemies, even *that* **enemy**--*especially* that one); feel gratitude, even when you're sure you are one angstrom away from losing everything you hold dear, or you have a big beef with God over unanswered prayers. The foundation of the basics, they all agree, is to joyously serve love to everyone, like a big-bosomed Italian mother with an overflowing platter of spaghetti and meatballs.

If you are not having the life you want but have plans to meet up with the Big Kahuna one day, the spiritual leaders urge you to check your basics, with particular emphasis on the serving up that platter of love.

I could not turn left or right without running into an essential basic in life. I was totally convinced of their importance so next I took a detailed look at what *my* basics in life were.

One of them is a short little morning ritual that keeps me centered for whatever the day will bring and helps keep the howling wolves of doubt and fear at bay.

As soon as I wake up I make myself a cup of tea and plop down on the living room sofa. After my ten-minute tea ceremony I meditate for 20 minutes and then I take five minutes to say my daily affirmations, a series of short, positive statements of how I want my life to be, worded as if the statements were already true. I have a book of three-by-five index cards on a metal ring. On each card I have written a positive affirmation and I say each one out loud like I mean it.

"Whatever I need, whenever I need it, for as long as I need it, will always be at hand."

"I release my hold on the past and its problems. I release all negative people. I say to them, 'I bless you. I forgive you. I release you from my life.'"

"I have terrific friends who challenge and stretch and love me. I stay connected to them and cherish the community I share with them."

"Today my heart is without fear."

"Every day in every way I am growing more prosperous."

"I live my life:
    Trusting the universe;
    Happy with what I have;
    Inviting all the good in;
    Letting the goodness in me emerge."

And, of course, I say, "I rejoice in the beauty and bliss that dance brings into my life."

I conclude my affirmations saying emphatically, "Something wonderful is happening to me today!" After this basic step I feel ready to meet the day.

Meditation and a tea ceremony aren't for everyone. Nevertheless, whether you realize it or not, you, too, have a set of daily basics, no matter how small or seemingly insignificant, that helps keep you centered. It's important to know what these basics are and give them the respect and commitment they deserve. Maybe you eat breakfast while you read the sports page...go for a run after work...write in your journal... walk the dogs... take your daily dose of Vitamin D... or talk to your fish or your ficus each morning. We all need those rituals—those basics—that keep us humming along, and when we neglect to do them, the day just doesn't feel quite complete.

Hey Mama: For All You Parents Out There

I have devoted the last 30 years to parenting and am boastful enough to say I am very proud of the end results. I believe the ultimate goal of parenting is to raise children into adults who can take care of and love themselves, work with and love others, and who respect the sanctity of life. How you do that depends on your basic steps.

From day one, without benefit of language, infants train us to meet their needs. When babies cry we immediately run down the list of potential causes: hungry, wet, dirty, colicky, lonely, bored? Hot? Cold? Newborns can communicate the most basic of the basics.

In a risky, bold move I asked my three grown children to reflect on what they perceived to be the basics of my parenting endeavor. They unanimously agreed on my values—which in turn inspired my parenting basics. Here's what they said:

BE KIND. One day we were talking about a TV newscaster who was breaking a great story. We watched as he mercilessly chastised the ignorance of one of the supposed experts on the show. While we three teenagers were impressed by the newscaster's intelligence to upstage the expert, you said you couldn't stand it and instructed us to change the channel. When we asked why, you said that someone could be the most talented, innovative, intelligent person in their field, but if they were arrogant and unkind you had no respect for them. You instilled in us that no matter what we pursued in life, kindness must be a basic tenet.

READ. You read to us relentlessly every day. We forgive you for reading us the book, Where the Red Fern Grows. *You had no way of knowing the dog dies in the end. Reading together gave us a love of words. We can't think of a better life skill to have.*

TRAVEL. You have taken us on trips all over the world and we are blessed with meaningful experiences in many cultures. When time and money was an issue you took us on a "camping trip" in the backyard. We enjoyed all our adventures.

RESPECT WOMEN. We grew up believing that women are just as capable, strong, spirited and intelligent as men. (We know you are adding "or more than.")

WORK HARD AND THINK BIG. We still hate you for the weed-pulling marathons, but we do have a good work ethic. You told each of us throughout our lives to dream big dreams. We are.

HAVE GOOD TABLE MANNERS. Eat with your mouth closed. Never use your finger to push peas onto your fork. No elbows on the table. Don't slurp your soup. Take small bites. We are now fully prepared for dinner at both the prom and Buckingham Palace.

I was surprised and delighted to find my kids' assessment right on. My basic steps of parenting are:

Be a compassionate human being above all else. Read yourself full. Travel and get to know the people on the planet you share. Respect women. Dream big dreams. Work your butt off.

And chew with your mouth closed.

I did laugh at one omission. No one mentioned a near-weekly staple: the dreaded Family Meeting, where the truth, in all its uncomfortable forms, came out. Every family has a basic communication style and, much to my children's horror, ours was *direct*.

As with every parent, my report card has lots of checks in the "needs improvement" column. My twenty-something children love to gather, open a bottle of wine, and remind me about things I'd like to forget. Apparently they still remember when I failed to pick them up on time after their activities, or how I embarrassed them, often by just breathing in and out. They love to expound in minutest detail the infinite number of opportunities I took to just generally screw up their lives. But no matter how often I failed to win the Good Parenting Seal of Approval, I knew if I just refocused on my maternal basics we all got back on track.

If you parent, you have basic guiding steps. One family told me theirs centered on connecting with nature. Whenever an issue in their household needed addressing, the family went outside to solve it. They walked on the beach, hiked up the mountains, and sat outside on the porch. Nature brought them back to a cohesive unit. Other families stayed aligned by attending church or temple, while still others reported using sports to teach their children about life lessons. I am not here to tell you what your basics should be, only to remind you to know what they are so you can keep doing them.

Committing to Your Basic Steps

I had the fabulous good fortune to have a roommate at age 54. My good friend, Melanie, was in transition, having moved quite suddenly from another state and she needed a place to land for a couple of weeks. The arrangement worked so well for both of us she stayed for nearly two years.

How did two middle-aged, strong-willed women have such a marvelous time together? From day one we committed to three basics. First, her two darling, non-shedding, obedient, totally lovable miniature schnauzer puppies must stay on the very comfortable lower level of the house. I have never owned a dog and having two puppies in my living room was my equivalent of seeing two head of cattle sitting on my beige chenille sofa. An irrational position to dog lovers, I understand, but this was an important basic for our harmonious co-habitation.

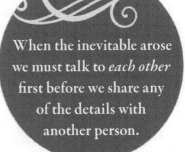

When the inevitable arose we must talk to *each other* first before we share any of the details with another person.

Secondly, we agreed not to formally split the cost of the groceries and we banned each other from uttering the words "my food and your food." Our reasoning went like this: We are not in college. When we are out of food, someone will go to the store. If one of us wants a certain item and worries the other of us might eat it, buy two. If we run out, the store is three minutes away. Neither of us eats all that much anyway. If one buyer feels the deal is lopsided, speak up. Chances are we'll be only a few dollars apart at the end of the month. As a result we'll spend less time going over grocery receipts, leaving more time to enjoy our meals.

Lastly, we acknowledged the obvious. We knew we could count on having concerns, issues, hurt feelings, irritations or better ideas of how to do things. We made a pact. When the inevitable arose we must talk to *each other* first before we share any of the details with another person. We are the only two who can actually fix the "problem". If I tell my friend how irritating it is that Melanie sometimes burns incense and she complains to her friend how mind-boggling it is that I talk out loud to myself, carrying on entire animated conversations like I have an imaginary friend (okay, I admit it, I do), what have we gained?

I am happy to say the dogs, Bella and Dolce, and I co-existed in mutual love and adoration. Truth be told, I liked being their alpha dog. Melanie and I ate like Parisians with nary a discussion about food costs and never did we break basic rule number three. We did have our occasional concerns and a couple of issues that required brave conversations, but they were compassionate discussions that we both were willing to have and that strengthened our relationship. (For the record, I did tone down my one-woman, emotive filibustering.) We are still best of friends because we agreed on our basics and demonstrated a true commitment to them. My friend, Chuck Canepa, mused that these three rules are good basic concepts for marriage. A wise man, Chuck.

Making Basic Steps Easy to Take

Using the concept of the basic step, in 2009 eight hospitals reduced their number of deaths from surgery by more than forty percent. This astounding result did not come from a new super-duper laser technology, a better surgical technique or even advanced training. The benefits were due to a strategy borrowed from the aviation industry: the lowly checklist.

In his best-selling book, *The Checklist Manifesto: How to Get Things Right*, surgeon Atul Gawande shows how applying this idea to the immensely complex world of surgery produced a 90-second checklist that reduced deaths and complications by more than one third in eight hospitals around the world--at virtually no cost and for almost any kind of surgery. The checklist focused on basic safety measures, such as ensuring that the patients got antibiotics to prevent infection and requiring that all members of the team introduced themselves. Knowing and sticking to the basics is nothing short of life-saving.

When I recognize that I am resisting what I know is good for me, I make myself a checklist and commit to using it.

We can use the checklist technique to focus on our own personal basics. When I recognize that I am resisting what I know is good for me and I want to get back on track in some area of my life I make myself a checklist and commit to using it. It might be a daily checklist:

1. Take two calcium tablets
2. Do 50 sit-ups
3. Floss
4. Eat five servings of fruits and vegetables

It might be a weekly basics checklist:

1. Balance bank account
2. Send a thank you note
3. Read at least 20 pages of the novel on my nightstand

Dr. Gawande says that a successful checklist is *short and doable.* A long and ambitious list begs to be resisted. Sending 15 thank you notes, reading 100 pages or doing 300 sit-ups--while these tasks will possibly make me a more conscientious friend and a smarter person with a more toned core--is not going to consistently happen. It's too much. A successful checklist also contains activities you really believe in. For instance, I like having one tooth in each spot in my mouth and flossing helps me keep it that way. The checklist differs from a to-do list because you have, in advance, *committed* to doing the items within specified time frames or parameters. They are not negotiable. Give this simple, yet powerful technique a try and see what happens.

Case in Point: Amazed and Amused

Karyn Buxman is the guru of applied humor, the study of the practical application of humor in everyday life. She is a much sought after "freaking funny" professional speaker, delighting audiences with her *I Have One Nerve Left and You*

Are Standing On It program. She used her unique brand of humor as a basic step to get herself through a difficult seven-year period.

Married, the mother of two sons and living in a small town in Missouri, Karyn first faced her youngest son's mysterious, totally debilitating and never-diagnosed headaches that baffled pediatric neurologists from coast to coast. She and twelve-year-old Adam used humor to cope with the interminable examinations. During one appointment the doctor asked Adam, "Do you ever experience "déjà vu?" and without missing a beat Adam retorted, "Didn't you just ask me that question?" Karyn said, "It took the doctor 20 seconds to get the joke while Adam and I were totally cracking up."

Karyn said her son's headaches provided a training ground for using humor as one of her basic steps. "We were still in full court press trying to solve Adam's migraines when I got a call from David, Adam's 19-year-old brother, who was a sophomore in college. He had gone to the student clinic with some chest pain, had an x-ray and a CAT scan and left with pain pills and instructions to follow up in 48 hours. The next day he called me with the news that he had mixed cell carcinoma of the chest. I could hardly breathe."

David had surgery and three months of cancer treatment. Prior to his illness he and one of his buddies worked part-time as bouncers at a college bar and were nicknamed Tonto and the Lone Ranger. Karyn continued, "David also used the basic of humor to cope. During his treatment he called to tell me his new moniker was 'Chemosabe.' I was with David helping him through the painful side effects when I got a call from my dad who asked, 'When can you come home? Your mother has Alzheimer's disease. I need your help.'"

"When I got home my mother pulled me aside and said, 'There are two men living in this house, your dad and a guy who looks exactly like him.'"

Karyn sighed deeply remembering her mother's comment. "I felt an enormous kick in the gut. My mother really believes there are two men here. I thought, 'How can this be possible? My mother is brilliant and accomplished. She's a pilot, into dancing, algebra, and calculus.'"

I smiled at her and said, "Well, Mom, here's what you do. When you see one of them say his name, 'LaMoine.' And if he answers, 'What Shirley?' that's Dad." And if the guy says, 'Who's LaMoine?' that's the other guy.' My mother and I could share this kind of humor. It was our saving grace. It helped ease my pain as I understood I was now an official member of the Sandwich Generation, simultaneously taking care of both my parents and my children."

All of these trials created a new problem: Years earlier as a young nursing student, Karyn had an intense desire to help people and fix them. "Unfortunately," she rued, "I looked high and low for a man who really needed fixing and I married him. Equally unfortunate was the fact that right now, with my family so ill, he was not the center of my universe and without my total devotion to what he needed, our marriage unraveled."

Her messy life was about to get messier. Karyn filed for divorce.

At this point in the story I asked her, "So then you went

to bed, pulled the covers over your head and stayed there for a year, waiting for the storm to pass. Right?" No, Karyn had other thoughts entirely--and a big dream.

"It took years but finally both boys were young healthy adults. Sadly, my mother had passed away. It was now my turn to take the next step for myself," she said. Leaving just about everything behind, including nearly all her money, she drove to San Diego to start a new life. The drive gave her three days to think. She pondered the lessons she'd learned in those trying seven years. What did she want now? The answer came quite clearly.

I wanted to live amazed and amused.

"I wanted to live amazed and amused," she said.

"I knew I had thrived because I had looked for the humor. And when I could not find anything funny, and truthfully much of it wasn't, I looked for what was amazing, the good and the bad."

As she drove mile after mile to a new adventure in California she understood that she had selected her first husband because he needed rescuing. She made a new list of qualities for her next husband (if there was to be one...).

"I wanted to fall in love with someone who was romantic, made me laugh, was romantic, lived near an ocean, was romantic, loved me back, and was romantic. My intention was pretty clear. And the Universe delivered ...I'd say in spades but more accurately, in hearts. Two years after I arrived in San Diego I married Greg Godek, the guy who wrote the mega best-seller *1001 Ways to be Romantic!*" (Who, by the way, also makes her laugh and lives three blocks from the ocean.)

When people hear her story they often ask, "Gosh, how did you do it?"

Karyn explained, "First of all, I did it out of necessity. I could not say, 'Hey, bummer about that cancer, but I'm really busy. Hope it all works out.' I felt responsible. When I got tired and discouraged, I thought, 'These are the steps I have to take. So step.'

When she focuses on intentions, hers are simply based on the belief that things will work out.

"I also did it out of love. I remember bargaining with God, pleading, 'Hey, these are just kids. Give these headaches and cancer to me. I've already had a cool life.'"

And Karyn admits to a sense of perseverance. She's a self-professed optimist. When she focuses on intentions, hers are simply based on the belief that things will work out. With this approach her steps became automatic. "Somehow", she said, "you know what you're supposed to do."

She's thrilled to report that she has a wonderful life now. She laughed, "My basic step is to live each day amused and amazed. Most of the time I am amazed and amused at good things, but I also use it, for example, on the California freeways saying, 'I am amazed that guy just cut me off like that in traffic or I am amused that someone could be so clueless.'"

Karyn knows there are plenty of next steps ahead for her. She said, "No matter what life holds for me I commit to my basic step of humor, marching forward amazed and amused."

Basics Run Deep

With the smugness of a prosecuting attorney who finally gets the guy whodunit to confess, let me end with this final example on the importance of sticking to your basics.

I read the New York Times bestseller, *How to Practice: The Way to a Meaningful Life,* by His Holiness, the Dalai Lama. Part One is entitled: *The Basics,* which he says are morality, meditation and wisdom.

I would guess everyone would agree on morality and wisdom. If you are trying to avoid meditation as a daily basic, may I gently suggest you give up on that idea? *Everybody* who is *Anybody* (Jesus, Buddha, Mohammed, Lord Shiva) says it's a must. The sole point of meditation is to make you more aware. My friend, Scott, explained it to me like this: Buddha was asked if he was a god or a prophet. The Buddha said, "No, I am awake." Scott hopes to distill his life mantra to that pithy line. "Plus, he added, "it would make for a great tombstone etching: 'He was awake. Now he's not.'"

Part Six of the Dalai Lama's book is entitled, "Steps Along the Way", which is (I wouldn't kid about this) a basics checklist for the path to enlightenment. Let me warn you, he says the path can take "eons and eons" to reach this illumed state of being. Pace yourself.

I think we can all safely take the hint. If His Holiness Himself thinks basics are the Way, my money is on him. To take the next step, know what your basics are and devote yourself to them. It will make all the difference. When stress creeps in, resist the temptation to stop. Focus on your basic steps and you'll find it much easier to move toward your dreams.

Accepting the Invitation

Dear Mary,

I like your idea about focusing on the basics. As a financial literacy advocate for women I have unfortunately seen so many people get in real trouble because they do not pay attention to their financial basics.

Money is funny. It plays a role in our lives every single day --either consciously or subconsciously. If you drank water from a cup, ate any kind of food, or blew your nose on a tissue... money played a role in bringing those items into your life. Over time, those series of interactions create a relationship between you and your money.

Sometimes the relationship is very clear-cut and stable. When you have a steady paycheck and things are going great, it may feel like being in a conga line at a wedding. Fun! Easy! Simple! At other times it can be very moody and gripping--the very same emotions you can feel when stepping out into a new stage of your life. The key to succeeding at either type of relation-ship is to never take your eyes off the basics.

When it comes to personal finance the three vital, basic steps are: (1) Living within your means, (2) Paying your bills on time, (3) Keeping on track with your retirement investments.

Let's start with living within your means--or "knowing your flow" as I like to say. Often times when a person is in transition or under stress they spend money on things and services to make themselves feel better. Pain and uncertainty can often accompany periods of stepping out (even stepping out into great, fun new things). As such, it can be easy to put your head in the sand when it comes to paying attention to what you are earning, spending or both. So the first step to staying in the groove is to make sure that as your life circumstances evolve your spending habits do as well. The last thing you need to do when undergoing a life transformation is to incur debt. A simple solution here is to carry around a small notebook --similar to a food journal. During your period of transition, commit to writing down every thing you spend. This simple step of connecting through the written word with your spending will heighten your awareness and assist you in making the spending decisions that best support your growth and happiness.

A second common misstep I see from people in transition is not paying their bills on time. It's easy to let this happen. These days it's the rare person that doesn't have at least 10 monthly bills to pay. Between cell phones, cable, Internet, gas, electricity, groceries, insurance, credit cards, water, rent/ mortgage, etc. it can quickly get away from you. While it may not seem like a big deal to let your bill paying habits slide while focusing on moving forward in a new area of your life, it can actually have grave financial consequences. See, we all have a 24/7 reality TV camera aimed at our wallets. It's powered by the big three credit bureaus (Equifax, Experian and TransUnion) and it's called a "credit score." A credit score is a three-digit number that summarizes how responsible you are with money. Unlike your weight, higher is better. Scores typically range from 300 to 850.

Why should you care? Because your credit score impacts all sorts of areas in your life. Banks will look at it to decide whether or not to lend you money to buy a home or a car. A landlord may look at it to decide whether or not to rent to you. Insurance companies may use it to determine how much to charge you for car insurance. Some employers may even use it to decide whether or not they will hire you. There are a variety of factors that determine your credit score but by far and away the biggest one is paying your bills on time. That single, basic step drives a whopping 35% of your credit score. A simple action step you can take is to move to online bill pay, where you automate alerts and payments, leaving nothing to chance.

Lastly, for many of us investing in the best of times can be tedious and overwhelming. Move into a period of transition and this is one financial move that many of want to stick in the closet. The most common mistake I see when someone leaves a job is not making a tactical decision about what they want to do with their retirement money (i.e. roll it over to an IRA, roll it into their new employer's plan, or keep it at their old employers). On top of this, the out of sight out of mind gene also has a tendency to kick in and people often leave those funds invested the same way they were when they left that job. The danger here is that you may have invested your retirement money in aggressive growth stocks when you started work in your 20s... but when you transition in your 40s or 50s you'd want a more balanced mix of investments. Getting frozen in your investment tracks is a classic move to avoid. A simple step you can take here is to visit with an hourly fee-based financial planner for an hour or two to decide what's the best course of action given your current circumstances. You can find an hourly fee-based financial planner at either NAPFA.org or GarrettPlanningNetwork.com.

You are right, Mary. Focusing on the basics, especially the financial ones, will make taking your next step so much easier and more joyful.
Sincerely,
Manisha Thakor

Author of *On Your Own Two Feet: A Modern Girl's Guide to Personal Finance*, and *Get Financially Naked: How to Talk Money with Your Honey*

———————⟨∘⟩———————

THE LESSON: *KEEP DOING YOUR BASIC STEPS*

Know what your basic steps are.
Find ways to make your basics easy to do.
Meditate.
Live amazed and amused.

Take Your Next Step

What are your most important basic steps?

Chapter Seven

Partner

Individually we are a drop. Together we are an ocean.
                                              --Ryunosuke Satoro

*F*red Astaire and Ginger Rogers were the quintessential ballroom dance couple. Ginger may have done everything Fred did, as is often quoted, only backwards and in high heels, but she could never have done that *alone*. Ballroom dancing requires a unique kind of partnership. It is not two people dancing together; it is creating a new oneness, something much greater than could be possible individually.

I remember watching the World Latin dance champions, Michael Malitowski and Joanna Leunis, perform. They entered the ballroom separately and strutted around the room. Then they united and it was like an explosion had gone off. They moved together in such unison, so into one another, it was like the rest of us were irrelevant. The energy they collectively exuded was palpable. It was clear they had made a mutual commitment to "take it higher."

In dance, you must create a connection with your partner. This is vital because without a connection, nothing, and I do mean *nothing*, happens. Why? Because without close connection you can't communicate with each other. You cannot be attuned to the constant feedback that is necessary. You miss all the important cues about how to meld your energies and simultaneously redirect them as a team.

Early on in my lessons I realized that one of the parts I enjoyed most was the sense of partnership I felt with both Manny and Taylor. They remain totally focused on me for the entire hour. No phone calls, texting, discussions with other instructors, or distractions of any kind.

I return the favor by being as devoted to them as a student could get. I hang on their every word and listen to every body language message. I admire, respect and feel grateful for their talent and professionalism. I love knowing that Manny was recently inducted into the Colorado West Coast Swing Hall of Fame and about the many students who win competitions with him. I am thrilled when I learn about Taylor, who routinely wins Best Teacher awards and along with his professional partner, Jennifer Corey, wins Rising Star awards at national competitions. It bonds us to each other as we share in our successes. My lesson is an amazing hour of genuinely paying attention to the essence of another human being.

Perhaps one of the most telling examples of the importance of partnering in dance is exemplified by *the invitation* to dance. There is a strict protocol to it because it creates the all-important connection necessary to dance well with your partner.

In the waltz, for example, the protocol first begins with eye contact. The man (leader) and the woman (follower) must really notice each other. Next, the man's left hand makes contact with the lady's right hand. They both feel their hands joined together. Then their bodies connect when the woman closes the gap. She is not pulled or arranged by the man. She is saying, "I am bringing my own energy to this union." The man then places his hand on the lady's back. This is the man's signal that he feels the position is good and he is ready to dance. The lady then places her left hand on the man's arm. This is the lady's signal that she feels the position is good and is ready to dance as well.

The theme is always, "Together we are better."

What makes the dance a true partnership is that both the man and the woman bring their own energy to the connection. It requires a compression that says, "Here I am. Do you feel my energy? I feel yours." Together their co-joined energies allow them to do things that would be impossible alone. They can create beautiful lines, do lifts and spins and tell a story by emotionally interacting with each other. The theme is always, "Together we are better." This kind of partnering in dance mirrors our basic human needs for love, intimacy and connection.

Say Yes, And...

Tina Fey, in her screamingly funny book *Bossypants,* also wrote about the co-joined energies that allow us to do things as partners that would be impossible to achieve alone. She explained "The Rules of Improvisation That Will Change Your Life and Reduce Belly Fat.[1]" The first rule she says is to always agree and *say yes*.

"When you are improvising, this means you are required to agree with whatever your partner has created. So if we're improvising and I say 'Freeze, I have a gun,' and you say, 'That's not a gun. It's your finger. You're pointing your finger at me,' our improvised scene has ground to a halt. But if I say, 'Freeze, I have a gun!' and you say, "The gun I gave you for Christmas! You bastard!" then we have started a scene because we have AGREED that my finger is in fact a Christmas gun." Fey is quick to point out that in real life we can't agree with everything everyone does. But her Rule of Agreement reminds us to "respect what your partner has created. Start with an open mind and a YES and see what happens."

Her second rule of improvisation is Say Yes, **AND**.

"You are supposed to agree and then add something of your own. If I start a scene with 'I can't believe it's so hot in here,' and you just say, 'Yeah...' we're kind of at a standstill. But if I say, 'I can't believe it's so hot in here,' and you say, 'Yes, it can't be good for the wax figures' ...or 'I told you we shouldn't have crawled into this dog's mouth,' now we're getting somewhere."

Her point applies to dance and life--since both are improvisations, too. *Always contribute.* Make sure you bring something positive to the party. Join forces to make the experience bigger and better. *Be a true partner.*

---

1 "Improv will not reduce belly fat."

Don't Try This By Yourself

I have spent my professional life sharing my philosophy: *Connection creates balance.*

I like to think I know something about this topic. When we get stressed we often disconnect from others, slipping into a prideful, "I can do this myself" mode. No, actually, you can't--not for long anyway. But even if you could, if somehow you alone were the exception to the No Man Is an Island rule, you'd miss the whole point of the human experience, which is the joy and ecstasy of partnering and making one plus one equal twenty-three.

For 15 years I was on faculty at a school of medicine doing cardiovascular research. One can hardly turn around without bumping into scientific studies that support the notion that if you want to happily and healthily take your next step in life, you'd better connect with some partners. Here are three of my favorite studies:

Dr. DG Blazer studied the effects of social support on 331 men and women aged 65 or over. Those who perceived their social support as impaired were *386 percent* more likely to die prematurely after only thirty months. Renowned researcher Dean Ornish, M.D., author of *Love and Survival,* wrote, "I am not aware of any other factor in medicine--not diet, not smoking, not exercise, not stress, not genetics, not drugs, not surgery--that has a greater capacity on our quality of life, incidence of illness, and premature death from all causes than love and intimacy."

It is not just a connection with humans that can make a big difference in our health and well-being. The Cardiac

Arrhythmia Suppression Trial studied men and women who had suffered a heart attack and had irregular heartbeats. Only one of the 87 people (1.1 percent) who owned dogs died during the study compared with 19 of the 282 people (6.7%) who did not own dogs--over six times as many! The love we feel for our four legged friends can heal us in ways no drug can.

In yet another research example of the power of connection Dr. John Gottman, University of Washington marriage researcher and author of *The Relationship Cure*, studied what he calls a connection "bid," a fundamental unit of emotional communication. A bid can be a question, a look, a touch, any single expression that says, "I want to feel connected to you."

He and his research colleagues studied the connection bids of married couples and discovered how profoundly the bidding process affects their relationships. The researchers discovered that husbands headed for divorce disregard their wives bids for connection 82 percent of the time, while husbands with stable relationships disregard their wives just 19 percent of the time. Wives headed for divorce act preoccupied with other activities when their husbands bid for their attention 50 percent of the time, while happily married wives act preoccupied just 14 percent of the time. Our ability and willingness to respond to our spouses' request for connection is a powerful predictor of marital stability and that stability is directly correlated to our health and happiness.

I could inundate you with tomes of research studies that prove human survival depends on our ability to make connections. It makes sense to tap into that power when we decide to take our next step forward.

The Short List

In the wake of the devastation from Hurricanes Katrina and Rita, I watched churches, charities, organizations and individuals step up and offer support. I sat and reflected on what I would do if I suddenly lost my home and all my material belongings. I was reminded of a concept I call "The Short List." In a time of personal crisis, who in your life would lend you a large sum of money--whether it is $500, $5000 or $50,000--without asking what the money is for and when they can have it back? Who would offer you a place to stay

If you are blessed with a Short List, perhaps now is a good time to let these individuals know how much you cherish them.

without an agreed-upon move out date? Who would take in your kids, pets or elders and do what's required to provide for them? I invite you to take a moment and jot down the people in your life who would meet these criteria. For most of us the list of individuals who would offer these things to us, is, well, a Short List.

Now the question is: How are you caring for these people, nurturing your relationships, and showing your gratitude for the depth of their commitment? Do you find yourself taking them for granted in the silent comfort that they will always be there for you no matter what? Do you sometimes give other less committed people more of your attention and concern? If you are blessed with a Short List, perhaps now is a good time to let these individuals know how much you cherish them. Be as good a partner to them as they have been to you.

Partnering with a Teacher

Our earliest recollections of moving forward in life involve our teachers. Perhaps right now a name comes to mind of that special instructor who made a difference in your life: Mr. Johnson who taught you to read or Mrs. Anderson who instilled in you a love of chemistry or Coach Smith who cut you from the team then worked with you after school to help you make the squad the following year. Dan Rather said, "The dream begins with a teacher who believes in you, who tugs and pushes and leads you to the next plateau, sometimes poking you with a sharp stick called 'truth.'" We are where we are today because of our teachers.

As adults, we continue to move forward to the next plateau because of the teachers we partner with today. I am learning many lessons about the power of partnering from one of my teachers, Sangay Wangchuk. Sangay is a wise, shaman-like Bhutanese travel guide whom I met in his homeland, the Kingdom of Bhutan. I have never met anyone who is more in tune with how nature and humans must partner to create a good life and keep the planet in balance at the same time.

One day as we hiked the Himalayas he told me a Bhutanese story about how vital it is that everyone have a teacher.

"A great monk learned all the secrets about mind control from his teacher. He started with the control of wind by learning

to levitate. *Next he learned to control fire, surviving on an icy mountain by regulating his own body heat. He tried to live without food and drink by fasting and meditating. The monk spent three years, three months and three days and mastered all these meditation steps to perfection. He passed his final test and returned to his village. He thought he knew everything there was to know and he abandoned his teacher.*

One day he saw a beautiful girl working in the field. He found a strange feeling going through his being. The monk thought that it was just a simple worldly sensation. He believed he could handle these urges himself. In the absence of his teacher, he did not understand the path his mind was taking. Without his teacher's insight and support he lost himself to the World of Five Delusions. He became the slave of Greed, Anger, Ignorance, Pride, and Jealousy. Thus he was back to the bottom of the valley once again. He could have avoided this fall from grace had he taken assistance from his teacher even when the subject looked simple."

> We need our teachers' eyes to see things about ourselves that we cannot.

Sangay and I had a wonderful discussion about this story. He told me that a teacher represents humility. To learn we must be humble. If we are too proud of our own knowledge we cannot learn. He said we need our teachers' eyes to see things about ourselves that we cannot.

I was struck by his wisdom because in that moment I realized that I am rewarded for acting as though I know everything. There are even those who suggest I should fake it until I make it. His advice is to instead humbly partner with teachers and never go without them.

Case in Point: From Where You Least Expect Them

Maryam Jordan was a 15-year-old girl living in Iran during its infamous 1979 revolution. Though she had liberal parents, the dangerous political climate convinced them an arranged marriage would be in her best interest and help keep her safe. Maryam was not in favor of this. She barely knew the proposed man, but she felt she had no choice but to obey her parents.

The marriage was a disaster from the start. She and her husband lived with his parents for three years. "I felt like a slave," Maryam said. "I was constantly watched, my husband was almost never home and I was stuck in the house working at my in-laws' beck and call."

One day, with an eight-month-old baby of her own now, her husband said to her, "Come with me. I want to show you something." Much to her horror, he introduced her to his pregnant mistress. Maryam said, "I was furious, terrified and did not know what to do. At first I kept this a secret from my family because I did not want them to lose respect for my husband. But when I finally did confess the truth, my parents immediately gave me an ultimatum: 'If you stay with your husband you will never see us again. Come home right this minute and we will support you and your son.'"

Maryam chose to leave her marriage, but to her grave disappointment the Islamic courts gave custody of their son to her husband and his family. She was granted visitation only every two weeks.

"Things in my family situation and in my country worsened. My parents told me I must immediately leave for the U.S. I protested vehemently because this would mean leaving my four-year-old-son. *This was unthinkable.* I was also scared, having never before left my country, not even on vacation. You have to understand. This was 1979 in wartime. The decision had been made for me. My father, who worked at the Swiss embassy, obtained visas for my 19-year-old sister Farah, my 28-year-old cousin Rashid, and me."

Maryam recalls what happened next. "We landed in Zurich with $1000 between the three of us. We hailed a taxi and, because of the obvious language barrier, we used hand gestures to tell the cab driver to take us to a hotel. He took us to one costing $300 a night and our money quickly evaporated. Rashid went to the nearby shopping center and asked everyone he met if they knew where he could find a Persian store."

He finally found an Iranian rug store and the owner who, after hearing their plight, offered to help in any way he could. The three travelers quickly learned that, although they'd been told otherwise, because of the poor political relations between Iran and America, getting a visa from Switzerland to the U.S. was impossible. Their only hope was to go to Spain and try to get into the country from there. So with the help of Maryam's father, who arranged for visas to Spain, they made their next plan. The rug merchant bought them each an airline ticket and gave them money for food and lodging until they could get on a flight.

They arrived in Spain with enough funds for one night at a hotel. After checking out the next morning the three of them sat on a park bench, with their luggage nearby. Maryam said, "We looked at each other and shrugged, '*now* what?'"

"At seven p.m., as dusk approached, my cousin told us to stay put and not to worry. Rashid said he was going for a walk through the park."

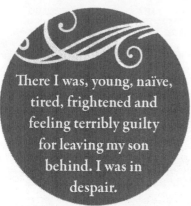

There I was, young, naïve, tired, frightened and feeling terribly guilty for leaving my son behind. I was in despair.

Thirty minutes later, her cousin returned with three young Iranian men. He had searched the park, listening for someone speaking his language. He told his fellow countrymen his story and they immediately offered to help. They moved out of their apartment and stayed with family so their new homeless friends had shelter. They also took Maryam, Farah and Rashid to the embassy to apply for a U.S. visa from Spain but once again they were denied.

At this point in their journey they were down to two choices: Apply for political asylum or go back to Iran.

Maryam said, "There I was, young, naïve, tired, frightened and feeling terribly guilty for leaving my son behind. I was in despair."

Together the trio decided to file for asylum and applied to the United Nations for help. The UN assisted them with an apartment, food, and a small financial stipend. They stayed in Spain for three months waiting for permission to enter the U.S. In that time Farah and one of the three men from the park, Faramarz, fell in love and made plans to reunite in America to get married.

"Finally", Maryam remembers, "I got the letter from the UN accepting my sister and me but my cousin was denied because he had a different last name and was not cleared to leave as part of our family group. Rashid had helped us so much and I refused to leave without him. But he insisted we go now and he would try to get to Canada as soon as he could."

On the day she and her sister left Spain, Maryam handed her cousin all the money the UN had given her. She had saved it for the trip but wanted Rashid to have it for his ticket to freedom when the time came.

Arriving in San Francisco she and her sister lived with their brother who had emigrated years before. Maryam spoke no English so she got a job as a maid at a motel.

"It was hard to adjust. Everything was so different, but you do what you need to do to survive." Maryam told me.

"I missed my son Reza terribly and set aside money so I could call him every month. But my in-laws were not supportive and even told his school principal that his mother had died. Without their consent it was difficult to stay in regular contact.

In the ensuing years, a now divorced Maryam remarried and had two more children. She attended college, graduated from beauty school and opened her own salon. When Reza was 18 years old Maryam helped him come to the U.S. to be with her. She and her son have worked hard to heal the rift that 14 years of separation causes.

I asked her who were her most important partners in her successful escape to a new life.

She answered, "My mom was key. For a long time I was angry with her for forcing me to leave Iran. But now I realize what she did for me. Mothers sometimes have to do the tough thing."

Maryam continued, "There were so many others. The rug merchant, the lady at the Swiss embassy who worked with my dad to get us a visa, my brother working behind the scenes and in particular, the United Nations personnel all played invaluable roles in helping me take my next step."

" But the ones I am most grateful to," she said, choking up, "are the three men in the park--Jamile, Kamy, and Faramarz. They rescued us at a time when we were out of options. On the day we were leaving for the U.S., Faramarz, my sister's fiancé, was also going to the airport to leave for Canada. The two lovers promised to somehow find a way to reunite in the U.S. and marry. Tragically, Faramarz was killed in a bus accident on the way to the airport. I truly believe he gave his life for us and I know he was on this earth to be our guide. I am grateful to him every day."

Maryam sighed, as if in relief and gratitude. "I hate to think what would have happened to me if I'd stayed in my marriage in Iran. I am enormously blessed to be here now. The amazing kindness of so many people made it possible."

Perfect Parnters: They're Everywhere

As we look for partners to help us take our next steps in life, just like Maryam, our important partners may come as a surprise. Here are just a few examples.

Nurses: Can't Live Without 'Em!

In chapter seven, *Keep Doing Your Basics*, I told you about a study in which doctors followed a simple checklist to save lives in the operating room. Dr. Peter Pronovost conducted an earlier study involving a checklist of the basics to insert a central IV line into a patient's artery. Dr. Provonost persuaded Johns Hopkins Hospital administration to authorize nurses to stop doctors if they saw them skipping a step on the checklist; nurses were also to ask the doctors each day whether any lines were to be removed, so as to not leave them in longer than necessary. This was revolutionary since the power hierarchy between doctors and nurses is firmly entrenched.

For a year Dr. Provonost monitored what happened. The results were hard to believe: The ten-day line-infection rate went from 11 percent to *zero*. Zero, as in nada. This one hospital calculated that in the next 15 months the nurses and doctors *partnering* on this checklist project had prevented forty-three infections and eight deaths and saved two million dollars in direct costs.

My right brain now invites your left brain to do the business math. If you go a step further and take the two million dollar savings and calculate in the additional *indirect* costs of, for example, lawsuits and increases in malpractice insurance—and then take THAT figure times the number of hospitals in the United States (nearly 6000) and then multiply THAT times just 5 years.... well...the total reminds me of a quip often attributed to the late US Senator Everett Dirkson, "A billion here, a billion there and pretty soon you're talking real money."

All I can say is, "Go, nurses, go.

Feng Shui: Partners Aren't Always People

I, too, found a surprise partner with astonishing results. When my roommate, Melanie, moved into her own house, she gifted me with the services of Nicolette Vajtay, a certified feng shui expert. Nicolette surveyed my home and then worked her simple magic, using the principles of this 5000 year-old Chinese art. We rearranged some furniture, moved art around, hung crystals, decluttered a bit and did a few chants. We turned the desk in my office on a slant to open myself to new opportunities and I got red silk sheets for my bed (self-explanatory). My 23 year-old son, Nick, watched all this with a cynic's eye. He grinned, "Are you doing this for giggles or do you actually believe this horse s--t?" At the time, I did not know the answer but I soon became a convert.

If I made a list of what we actually physically changed it would be minor, but the results were anything but. Let me say it was one of the top ten most amazing things I have ever experienced. The chi flowed so much it made the drapes move. Family and friends alike commented on the difference. House guests wanted to know what brand of mattress they'd just had their best ever night of sleep on. I was so full of energy I was up at 4 am painting an interior wall in the garage Barn Red. You would have thought Nicolette had sprayed an air freshener of Ecstasy and we were all inhaling deeply.

And now? You could not pay me to move anything back. The house feels so good. (And yes, she does very effective Skype video consultations.) But the point is not that I want you to feng shui your home or office. (Actually, I do think you should, but it's not the point.) The point is, when you are moving forward, keep an open mind to whom your important partners might be. They may come from unexpected places.

Masterminds: Two Brains Are Better Than One (And Seven Brains Are Even Better)

Napoleon Hill, author of the classic, Think and Grow Rich, had a lot to say about the power of partnering. He considered partnering a kind of mastermind that he defined as "coordination of knowledge and effort, in a spirit of harmony, between two or more people, for the attainment of a definite purpose." He believed that not only was it an economic advantage to connect with a special group of individuals, but that there was a psychic phase of the mastermind principle as well. He wrote, "No two minds ever come together without, thereby, creating a third, invisible, intangible force, which may be likened to a third mind." In a 254 page book that uses very few exclamation marks, Dr. Hill used one to end this sentence regarding the mastermind: "Great power can be accumulated through no other principle!"

> "No two minds ever come together without, thereby, creating a third, invisible, intangible force, which may be likened to a third mind."

I have two mastermind groups. One is physical, an amazing collection of seven colleagues who serve on "my board" guiding me on strategic business decisions.

I will confess (at the risk of making my friend, Kris, squint and wrinkle her forehead again) that I also have a "mental" mastermind group made up of people, some living, some not, none of whom I have ever met, who I ask for help in my creative projects.

The committee members of this latter group change depending on the task, but "regulars" include TV pioneer Steve Allen, author Erma Bombeck, and comedian Stephen Wright (who wrote lines such as "I drive way too fast to worry about cholesterol" and "If toast lands butter side down and cats always land on their feet, what happens if you strap toast on the back of a cat and drop it?")

I ask for their input often and feel confident their collective creative genius helps me. One day, for example, I was typing along about how unrealistic we are to think we can get it all done. I said to my comedic partners, "Hey, this is getting kind of staid. Write something witty." The next thing I know, I've typed, "Wearing clean underwear every day is an overrated concept." And then came the line, "Even our Wonder bras have a limit to the miracles they can perform." I do not know who sent these lines but I am sure I did not write them. These quips may not be quite as clever as, "Do you think that when they asked George Washington for an ID he just whipped out a quarter?" I consider Stephen Wright a prime suspect. Thank you, Stephen.

If you, too, are now on Kris's side and wrinkling *your* forehead, you may want to re-read Chapter Two. Remember that quarks do funny, funny things that totally go against our long-held beliefs about how information is transmitted. Quantum physics researchers have proven mathematically that **everywhere there is a ceaseless passing back and forth of information that is irrelevant to time and space.** Even if you are not a believer, you might want to give this creative mental mastermind method a try. It's free, non-radioactive and low-fat. It can't hurt.

The Story of the Four Harmonious Friends

My wise teacher, Sangay, told me one of the many versions of the famous Bhutanese parable about the Four Harmonious Friends: the elephant, the monkey, the hare and the bird. As the story goes, each of these animals helped a banyan tree grow. The bird dropped the seed into the ground as it flew over fertile soil. The hare watered it. The monkey fertilized it. The elephant stood by and protected the young sapling. Together their individual contributions made the tree grow large, so tall, in fact, that none of them could reach the fruit. So together they made a pact. The monkey stood on the elephant's back, the hare stood on the monkey's back and the bird stood on the hare's back. The bird could now reach the higher branches and with her beak she picked the fruit and passed delicious food to all of them. Working individually they created a success, but they could not reap the rewards. Working as a team they easily had all they needed and more.

With apologies to the Bhutanese scholars, for me this story begs the question, "Who's got your back? And whose do you have? Do you exist in a culture of harmonious cooperation? How will you create your own unique partnerships to go forward and take the next step in your life?

Accepting the Invitation

Dear Mary,

Seven pounds, 11 ounces. ten fingers. Ten toes. Perfect in every way. With a fuzz of strawberry blond hair, my daughter, Carrie Ann, arrived into the world letting the nurses know she was a force to be reckoned with. It would have been impossible to believe, as I held this newborn infant in my arms, marveling at her perfection, that she would not live to her eighteenth birthday. On December 19, 1998, seventeen-year-old Carrie Ann died suddenly and unexpectedly from epilepsy.

Thus I began a journey with a very high price and one that I did not have the skills to take.

I was leveled to a parking lot. At first I couldn't eat or drink, brush my teeth, get a good night's sleep, bathe or even dress myself without direction and encouragement. Formulating a cognitive thought was nearly impossible. Everything that used to be second nature seemed totally foreign. I wasn't entirely sure I wanted to live.

This is a familiar scenario for many who have lost loved ones, suddenly or not. I now understand that this journey cannot be taken alone, though many try. Isolation becomes a black hole and we can sink deeper and deeper, often complicated by well-meaning others who don't know what to say or do as we withdraw and refuse to participate in life. My three F's, family, friends and faith, held me together.

I learned that if we are lucky enough it is our true friends who sweep in and take us by the shoulders, guide us around and tell us what to do. In time they move back to take care of their own lives and we are left to move forward, looking for new ways to take the pain away, believing what people say is true, "Time heals all wounds." I vehemently do not agree with this. I think if we depend strictly on time we will just practice new and different ways to take the pain of grief away, stuffing and suppressing it, until it eats at our physical body. As a result, we look for ways to anesthetize our pain. We try to sleep it away. We might try to drink, drug, gamble, exercise, or shop it away. We would do just about anything to distract ourselves from the relentless, searing pain. I tried many of them.

Moving forward often requires us to first revert backward, to find the things that we know to be true in our lives. For some we find the truth in our faith. Others enter a period of deep questioning, re-examining what they once believed, and looking for meaning. Then we begin again at square one, with a new truth, searching for a new normal.

Each person will grieve in his or her own way. No matter how we go about it, we must surround ourselves with people who love us and who will walk this journey unceasingly with us. It could be our four-legged companion who gives us a reason to put one foot in front of the other, providing unconditional love.

It was not until I began my own grief work that my transformation and reconciliation of loss began. I made progress when I partnered with God, my counselor, and my circle of *loving family and friends. I joined a group called Compassionate Friends, for parents who have lost a child. It is a club no one wants to be a member of, but if you are, their unconditional support is priceless.*

Inspired by what I experienced I am now a grief counselor, partnering with others at a time of their deepest need. I am honored to walk the journey of grief with them and elated to watch them emerge as they find new hope, meaning and purpose.

It is hard to tell someone who is newly bereaved that they will find blessings out of loss, but I have found many. It is hard to tell someone newly bereaved that they will find joy and happiness again, possibly in greater magnitude than before. I certainly have. I'm married to my wonderful new husband, Chris, who understands that my grief is woven into the fabric of who I am. What joy he brings into my daily life! My daughter, Niki and her husband, Andy, have given me the two cutest grandchildren in the world and I have the eight- by- ten glossies to prove it. After three tours of Iraq, my son Branden, married Juliessa, the love of his life. And of course, my beautiful Carrie will stay ever present in my heart.

In gratitude,

Linda Coughlin Brooks

Grief Counselor

Greenwood Village, Colorado.

lcoughlin@griefandgrowth.com

THE LESSON: *PARTNER*

Accept that humans are better together.
Take care of your Short List.
Humbly embrace your teachers.
Partner in harmonious cooperation.
Say yes, and...

Take Your Next Step

Who would you like to partner with?

Chapter Eight

Fail

Fall seven times. Stand up eight.
--Japanese proverb

My dance instructor, Taylor, is a stickler for technique, and Lordy, there is a lot of it in ballroom dancing. Take the very difficult foxtrot, for example. The dance begins with a specific hold. When we practice this dance Taylor demands a near perfect frame. He coaches, "Stretch-stretch-stretch-stretch-stretch, come on, more! more! more!... s-t-r-e-t-c-h... while he holds me in his arms and waits for me to fire up my core muscles, drop my lats in the back, tense my entire body like I have the world's tightest buns of steel, elongate my neck to increase the distance between my ears and my shoulders, and tilt my head to the side as if I am looking around a tree in the park to see where my toddler just ran off to. My arms are in the UFO position (up, forward, out) and they lay on him like I am dancing with a porcupine. My legs are bent and balanced, with energy flowing down through the floor and past the earth's crust to the center of our planet. I place my weight over one foot, simultaneously lifting both my pelvic muscles and the skin on my forehead as high as I can. (I am not kidding.) At this point I have burned 2200 calories and we have not even started dancing yet.

There are, as you can see, a lot of moving parts to this dance, meaning many, many things can go wrong. Most of the hour lesson is filled with mere moments of getting it right. I do have good days on which the Foxtrot God smiles down on me. But just when I have reached a new level of competence, Taylor, like the excellent coach that he is, ups the pressure, pushing me to do even better, which means at first I do it even worse...which brings us to the topic of failure.

Fear, Failure and Moving Forward

Sorry, Houston, but actually, as we take our next step in life, failure is an option. A given. A necessity. Still, I will confess

I did not want to write a chapter called "Fail." I wanted to call it "Overcoming Temporary Setbacks." But my daughter, Sarah, admonished me, "Why sugar-coat it? You should call it 'Fail' because that is what it is. What's so wrong with that?" Sir James M. Barrie, the creator

of Peter Pan, agreed with her when he said, "We are all of us failures. At least the best of us are." But how does failure relate to taking our next step?

As we take our next step in life, failure *is* an option. A given. A necessity.

The prevailing advice on failure is not to fear it. Ha. That is like saying, "Don't fear the pain of childbirth, even if your last labor took three days and the doctor finally had to back up the tractor and use chains to deliver your bundle of joy. Just breathe through it and you won't remember the agony." These words of wisdom come from people who think women have very, very small brains. I got news for 'em. We remember it. Each and every contraction. Likewise, we remember each and every time we fail, too. Amnesia is rare when it comes to our downfalls. Given most of our experiences with it, fearing failure seems logical. But is there a way to use fear of failure to our advantage? I decided to thoroughly research both of these "f-words."

I first researched fear, from A--including Aeronausiphobia, which is the fear of vomiting due to airsickness, (which sounds like a pretty reasonable fear to me and one you might not want to be cured of) to Z—as in Zemmiphobia, the fear of the great mole rat. I am not sure how you develop that fear but it sounds even worse than the fear of failure, which is called Atychiphobia. The world, according to my research, is full of things to be afraid of, and failure is near the top of the list for many of us.

Next, I took a swing at what the experts had to say about failure. Much of what was written is true; all innovation first involves failure, and many of these examples come from the world of business. From Apple to Amazon, from Target to Toys 'R' Us, successful companies and organizations are looking for ways to encourage creative risk-taking and to reward such behavior. I was encouraged to "fail small and succeed big," "learn the challenging secret to successful failure," and "fail early, fail fast, and fail often." The latter advice made me wonder if the authors had been watching my foxtrot lessons.

I was not sure what to do with all this cheery advice on failure. I hate to fail. Failure is about as self-esteem-building as winning the prize at the annual Ugly Christmas Sweater party, three years running. I got some insight, however, when I read the acclaimed book, *Feel the Fear and Do It Anyway*. According to author Dr. Susan Jeffers, it is *not* the fear of failure that keeps us from stepping out and realizing our dreams. She reasons that "if everybody feels fear when approaching something totally new in life, yet so many people are out there 'doing it' despite the fear, then we must conclude that fear is not the problem."

Some fearful people find the risk of failure irrelevant to their plans while other fearful individuals become paralyzed at the thought of risking it. The difference between the two groups, she says, is how they *hold* the fear. The former group holds their fear from a position of power (choice, energy and action), and the latter holds it from a position of pain (helplessness, depression and paralysis). Her conclusion is not to wait until you are no longer afraid. *You are going to be afraid.* The paradoxical trick to overcoming your fear of failure is to feel the fear and do it anyway. Just keep moving forward–kind of like doing your basic steps.

Do You Know Why?

One way to stay on course when failure rears its helpful head is to remind yourself why you set your original intention in the first place. Why is it worth risking failure? Why do you want to feel the fear and do it anyway?

An audience member at a speech I gave to the American Medical Association taught me a lesson about asking why. I gave a presentation on connection and life balance, then asked the doctors how they planned to use the information in my program to get more connected with what was really important to them.

Some said they would carve out some time for their passions. Others planned to focus more on their families. From way in the back of the room a young doctor raised his hand and announced, "I'm going to get married in 18 days."

I exclaimed, "Wow! All because of this seminar? That's amazing. Do you think you can find a bride in that short of a time frame?"

Actually, it turned out, the wedding, including the bride selection, was already in the works.

He said, "I have to admit that a part of me has cold feet. I keep asking, 'Am I doing the right thing?' I realized my fear was simply because in the midst of the wedding hubbub, our love for each other had gotten lost in the details. I am going to sit down with my fiancé, reconnect and tell her all the reasons *why* I am marrying her."

Some attendees laughed and others nodded in agreement in an emotional response to their colleague's brave confession of the primal fear he had of risking failure. Here he was, on the brink of this major step forward- a step he had committed to, wedding rings and all- *for the rest of his life*. He wanted to know if he was about to make a huge mistake. To answer this question he wisely asked himself, "Why? Why do I want to overcome this fear of risking failure?"

This question is one we can all use when we are facing our next step forward. When what you are afraid of seems very real, when the voice in your head asks over and over, "Am I doing the right thing?" just stop and ask yourself why. Why am I adopting this child? Why am I quitting my perfectly good job to start my own business? Why did we decide to downsize and move to the country? Why is it a good idea to move his mother in with us?

A few hours after my speech, as I sat on the plane home, I reflected on the doctor's question, and his assessment about having "gotten lost in the details." It occurred to me-don't we all suffer from that occasionally? We get so focused on the who-what-where-when that we lose sight of the why--and fear builds. **When confusion and the inevitable temporary setbacks happen, we can move through them more easily when we understand our *why*.**

Case in Point: Just a Bubba with a Good Idea

Kent Taylor's love affair with the restaurant business started in college when he waited tables and bartended at TGIFridays, followed by stints as a nightclub manager and pub owner. He then joined Bennigans's in Dallas, where he approached the CEO with the new business ideas he had swirling in his mind. He was promptly reassigned to Denver, far from headquarters, where he would hopefully not cause any more trouble.

Kent was always full of new innovative concepts. His favorite idea was for a "cowboy steak house" and he enthusiastically pitched several well-known restaurant investors but was always shot down.

Next, he joined Kentucky Fried Chicken as an area manager. With KFC's parent company PepsiCo preaching innovation, Kent took that message to heart and began experimenting with chicken fingers and sandwiches. He set up his store as the "KFC of the future" with these company un-endorsed items. When his regional manager brought an entourage of top KFC officers through on a store tour, the "you-know-what hit the fan," he recalls. He had crossed forbidden lines and he was told in no uncertain terms that his job was in question.

That night he pulled out his old concept binders. He began pitching his ideas again to anyone who would listen, but he received rejection after rejection. Finally, after six long years of chasing his dream, he met with a man who agreed to finance a concept they called Buckhead Bar and Grill. However, after a couple of months of soft sales they stopped serving lunch, as Kent was unable to physically maintain the 100 plus hours he was working. When sales got even softer, he applied for a general manager position at Outback Steakhouse and the Olive Garden but was promptly turned down. With debt mounting it appeared Kent's dream was just one or two months from failure.

Creatively salvaging what he could, he got $20,000 from his partner, spent half paying bills and used the other half to convert the restaurant into a local pub, with good results. Sales increased, and after three months Buckhead Bar and Grill was back in business.

He and his partner planned to open another Buckhead but could not agree on terms. Devastated by this turn of events Kent knew he had two choices: Stay 100 percent with Buckhead or develop his own ideas. Kent hit the pavement once more.

He put together another 20 investment packages and again he was turned away. It was a tough time. He was single-parenting his two young daughters and living with his parents to make ends meet. It was about this time that his father suggested maybe he should "work for a nice company with good benefits." So he went back to Buckhead to try again, but his burning obsession flared up and resulted in his creation of ten more investment packages. Unfortunately, the story was the same: no takers.

One night one of his friends introduced him to a buddy, Dr. John Rhodes, sitting at the bar. Kent bought him a beer and showed John his dream drawn on cocktail napkins. John expressed interest and soon he and two of his other physician partners invested $300,000. At last, after years of dreaming and scores of refusals, the doors opened at his first "cowboy steak house" in Clarksville, Indiana.

Kent quickly opened four more stores and then, in yet another blow, within the year three of them were failing. Unable to pay bills Kent divided all invoices into three desk drawers:

Drawer one: "Squeaky Wheels." Must-pay invoices;

Drawer two: Companies that do not hound, but want their money as soon as possible;

Drawer three: Companies who don't mind waiting for their money; there may be up to five unpaid invoices on one check.

At the same time that three of his five stores were failing, in what can only be described as unending faith, Kent was still creating. He wrote his mission statement, "Legendary Food, Legendary Service." He developed an Upside Down Organizational Structure Pyramid, the Top Ten Food Priorities and the Top Ten Service Priorities. He even hired a new chef to improve the menu.

When the first of his three failing restaurants closed in Sarasota he looked for the bright side. His Gainesville restaurant was in desperate need of a new air conditioning unit. The guests were fanning themselves with menus and the kitchen staff froze towels to put under their hats and took their breaks in the walk-in cooler.

So, in the middle of the night, Kent went to the closed Sarasota store and crane-lifted the recently purchased AC unit from the roof and installed it in the Gainesville store. The next day his guests were delighted and his staff came out of the cooler.

He was so confident in making it big one day that, just one year after the third store closed Kent dressed up as Santa at the company Christmas party and gave each of the original Clarksville managers a bottle of Dom Perignon to be opened when the restaurants went public.

At this point of his story I stopped and reexamined the

facts of his business endeavors. I thought to myself, "This guy does not know the meaning of the word failure." Those who know him well say he does not know the meaning of many other words either, such as *no, can't, give up* and *sleep*, to name just a few.

Kent is a bit of an enigma, as many visionaries are. For the first few years his business card did not include a title. Tall, trim, handsome, and youthful, Kent describes himself as "just a Bubba with a good idea." I would add, "and with perseverance, business savvy, an endless devotion to his restaurant family and his ideals." This Bubba is the founder of the Texas Roadhouse, which now has more than 350 stores in 46 states and one in Dubai. The Texas Roadhouse chain has won dozens of awards, including #1 Steakhouse in America and *Consumer Reports* Best Value and is ranked in the top 40 on the *Forbes'* Best Small Companies list. Six years after receiving their Christmas gift of champagne, the original Clarksville managers traveled to Wall Street to mark the moment when the company did indeed go public. Later they celebrated at Kent's home and poured the bubbly.

The casual restaurant chain is renowned for its hand-cut steaks, made-from-scratch-sides and fresh-baked breads. And I have to tell you; this cowboy steakhouse establishment wins my award for the best fall-off-the-bone ribs you'll ever eat. This is all quite an accomplishment for a company that not so long ago used the Three Drawer Invoicing system.

I asked Kent to enlighten me about his views on failure. "Were you ever afraid of failure?"

"Never," he said emphatically. "The possibility of it just makes me work harder. In high school if I asked a girl for a date and she said no, I'd ask her three more times. I guess I just have weird wiring."

"That is not to say," he continued, "that I wasn't devastated when the three stores failed. It was really tough financially and my investors bailed. But I figured out what I did wrong. When I got the answers I used that information to make my other stores even better."

Kent does not keep his failures a secret. He said, "I have three mementos on my office wall: two $500,000 fish and a $400,000 steer skull, mounted and framed with the date of each of the three store closings." He assigned each of them these dollar values because that's how much his company lost in those markets after he chose bad store locations. He said he looks at them when he's making real estate decisions. "The mountings are daily reminders," Kent said, "not to get too cocky."

Next I asked him about the relentless rejections. "What did you feel about all those who said no? Did you feel they failed you?"

"Not at all," Kent replied. "I had to look at the man in the mirror. Frankly, my business plan was not good enough to invest in. I was responsible for revising it, and I am glad for the rejections so I was forced to do that."

I was still curious about how anyone could keep going with so many downturns. I asked, "Did you ever have dark days when you thought it might be time to throw in the towel?"

Kent laughed. "Tons of dark days. Money was a huge issue. I actually borrowed money from my two little girls' piggy banks for their school lunches and left them IOU slips. But I have always been a driven person, dating back to my track days in high school and college. During the really hard times I read every real estate and business book I could get my hands on and I listened to hours of motivational tapes. I was constantly seeding my brain with positive propaganda. I believe the key to my success was persistence and I framed Calvin Coolidge's quote and hung it on my wall so I can see it every day."

The words clearly hold a special place in Kent's heart because he then read them to me, slowly, line by line, instructing me to write each one down. I felt I was sitting at the feet of a master and I did as I was told:

Nothing in the world can take the place of persistence.

Talent will not. Nothing is more common than unsuccessful men with talent.

Genius will not. Unrewarded genius is almost a proverb.

Education will not. The world is full of educated derelicts.

Persistence and dedication alone are omnipotent.

The slogan "press on" has solved and always will solve the problems of the human race.

--Calvin Coolidge

It could be a poem entitled, "Kent Taylor."

His confidantes say this brilliant entrepreneur might one day just suddenly sell it all and become a boat captain and a ski bum. Maybe so, but I bet he'll be scribbling new wacky ideas on a cocktail napkin up until the day he meets up with the Big Restaurateur in the Sky. No doubt Kent will be pitching Him ideas as well.

Is It Really "Failure"? Or Is It...*Success*?

My view of failure crystallized during a visit to Bali. One afternoon I decided to take a surfing lesson. Feeling quite confident, I crawled on the board, eager to stand up and show the world that I could surf.

But each time I stood, I fell. The frustrated Balinese instructor kept trying to coach me, but wave after wave I "failed." A few times I just rode the board to the shore, lying flat on my belly or sitting on my knees. I giggled like a schoolgirl, feeling the power of the ocean lift my board and propel me over the wave's crest. And in the exhilaration of the cloudless sky, and the warm, azure water I had an epiphany: Why must I stand up? Trying to stand up and falling was not nearly as much fun as just effortlessly riding the board to shore. It dawned on me--I was here to have a good time! It made me stop and think of the myriad of ways I'd let others set the bar of accomplishment.

Sometimes we are driven to succeed and worry about failing without really asking ourselves if we know what success means to us.

So what if everyone around me was standing on his or her board? Sometimes we are driven to succeed and worry about failing without really asking ourselves if we know what success means to us. Here I was, fortunate enough to be in a beautiful, exotic part of the world with family that I love. Might that be enough--actually more than enough--to delight me? What did standing up have to do with it? Why did I label my experience a failure?

So I'd like you to ask yourself, "Do I set my own goals?" *Have you pondered recently what success and failure mean to you?* Do you want the promotion to management, or do you actually love the client contact or the technical side of the business better? Do you really want another child? Would the house you live in actually be more comfortable than financially stretching for a bigger one with a longer commute simply because you can afford it? Would your ego let someone new take a turn at chairing the community event? What if you recognized that sometimes it is actually more rewarding to just lie down and enjoy the ride?

What if you are not failing at all— you are succeeding?

What if, in fact, "failing" (to stand up on that board, to spend more money than you have, to take a stressful job...) actually means that as far as your intention goes, *you are not failing at all—you are succeeding?*

I grew up in an era in which I was taught that Father Knows Best. Doctors, priests, the government, the Supreme Court, pediatricians, teachers and husbands were the experts. Even the ads for hair coloring warned, "Only your hairdresser knows for sure."

Actually, those all turned out to be lies--not in the sense that people prevaricated (though some did), but in the sense that what they spoke was *their* truth, not mine.

Trust your own instincts. Be sure that the next steps are the ones *you* want to take and that the criteria for determining whether something represents a success or a failure originate with you.

Failure and Mastery: Two Sides of the Same Coin

I accept that I will sometimes fail as I take the next step, but I want to go on record that I prefer immediate and sustained mastery. Sometimes when I fail to get a dance move correct after repeated attempts, I stomp up and down, especially when I had the move just a minute ago and then I lost it. I do, however have a strict policy: No angry outbursts and no crying at dance class. I save those tantrums for when I am running very late and find myself queued up behind the person with 59 items in the 12-items-or-less line.

Failure and mastery go hand in hand because if we didn't want to strive for more, there would be nothing at which to fail. I am reminded of the story of a soldier the night before he went on his first mission. He confided to his sergeant that he was scared. His superior got in his face, eyeball-to-eyeball, and yelled, "Soldier, if you ain't scared of it, it ain't big enough."

Perhaps one of the best examples of the successful marriage of failure and mastery is Steve Jobs. Following his death he was lauded, quite correctly, as a true technological genius who revolutionized the world. And yet he believed that his failures were directly responsible for his mastery. In his now famous commencement address at Stanford University Jobs said, "I didn't see it then, but it turned out that getting fired from Apple was the best thing that could have ever happened to me. The heaviness of being successful was replaced by the lightness of being a beginner again, less sure about everything. It freed me to enter one of the most creative periods of my life... Sometimes life hits you in the head with a brick. Don't lose faith. I'm convinced that the only thing that kept me going was that I loved what I did."

Our intentions hold big promise, infinite possibilities. So, yes, we will by necessity fail. How could we not be afraid? Go ahead. Do it anyway.

Accepting the Invitation

Dear Mary,

Years ago I learned a profound lesson about failure from an unknown man whom I never really even met.

First, let me tell you a bit about myself. In 1975 I left New Hampshire for college with a pocketful of values based on years of Boy Scouting, civic involvement, and my mother, who was a strong advocate for the less fortunate. In college, as president of the student senate, I organized Vietnam war protests and challenged the administration for what I considered to be flawed academic policies. My focus was on doing what I thought was right, born from a deep passion for justice.

What followed was a remarkable career. By age 37, I was the president and CEO of a company owned by a publicly traded corporation. I accomplished many business goals, had a house with a swimming pool, a large sail boat a short walk from my house on a peninsula of the Chesapeake Bay, and a membership in a prestigious private Baltimore business club. I had a wonderful wife, an infant son, and what seemed like life on a string. Or, so I thought.

Fail

Within a couple of years I began to be aware of an uneasiness that, while not entirely foreign to me, had always disappeared with each new step on the corporate ladder or purchase of some new toy. But this time, there were no new rungs to climb or toys to buy. I had no idea what to do about my uneasiness, so I simply did what I had been doing: run fast and not think about it. Then I met him.

It was early one morning in the spring of 1994 and I was late for a meeting. Tearing through the back streets of Baltimore in an expensive sports car, I was focused on getting to the meeting with clients in the hopes of increasing our business with them. From the corner of my eye, I saw a man lying face down in a filthy gutter on an empty street, with no one around and no house nearby that might have been his home. He looked like he was just another drunk or drug addict passed out, the result of his habits. To me, it was not a big deal, just a guy who was getting what he deserved, a guy who ought to understand there are consequences to the things we do in life.

Three blocks went by and then, BANG. It wasn't a shot from a gun; it was a shot from my conscience that startled me. My heart raced and I began to sweat. All the lessons of my earlier life tore off their shrouds and reminded me that I had just driven by a human being whose life could be slipping away. What was worse, I hadn't cared. After all, it was his own fault, I thought. I did manage to call 911 several blocks later. But my body and mind had gone tilt with the harsh awareness of how far I had fallen from my core values. I had become, it turned out, seduced by privilege and driven by success, so much so that I no longer felt another's pain. My definition of success had

187

now been formed by how others responded to people of wealth, status and power.

This John Doe had shaken my Etch-a-Sketch and erased the pretty picture I had of myself. I had come face to face with my own failure to live up to the values I held dear. The shot to my conscience allowed me to really take stock of who I was and who I wanted to become. The man I had numbly driven by had forced me to admit my confusion and confess that, for all my visible self-assurdedness, I was faking it.

I knew I needed to wake up and build a different life. I became increasingly disillusioned with many of my company's business practices and the insatiable appetite to make money. My success at work held odd paradoxes. I was struck by the fact that, in order to satisfy shareholders and my bosses, I needed to lay-off many people, mostly midlevel staff and the lowest income earners; all the while the very people who had, for years, made the strategic decisions that led the company to its fiscal nadir were reaping bonuses and continued employment. Within the year, I resigned my dream position, a confused forty-one year old man, more uncertain and more unclear than anything I could have imagined.

But I have since found my way. I have for the last five years served as CEO of Horizons, a non-profit organization, serving seniors, children, families and the economically disadvantaged. This position has allowed me to combine my business philosophy with the broader compassion I hold for the life struggles that many people experience, often through no fault of their own. And now, my newest adventure begins in August when I move to Nashville, to enroll in the Masters Degree program in Theological Studies at Vanderbilt University.

While being asleep at the wheel those many years ago felt like a failure to me at the time, I now believe that the man lying in the gutter was a gift to me. I have a new definition of failure--living inauthentically. I may make mistakes but as long as I strive to live an authentic life I will see my life as a success. I have woken up.

People often ask me whatever happened to that man and whether my phone call saved his life. I don't know those answers and never will. But what I do know is that call might have saved mine.

Thanks for the interesting discussion on failure.
Sincerely,
W. Scott Jamieson
Masters of Theological Studies Candidate, 2012
Vanderbilt University

THE LESSON: *FAIL*

Feel the fear and do it anyway.
Know your "why."
Define your own success.
Persist.

Take Your Next Step

Specifically how might you fail in taking your next step?

Chapter Nine

Practice

A knowledge of the path cannot be substituted for putting one foot in front of the other.

--M.C. Richards

*T*hree months after I began lessons at Booth's DanceSport studio in Denver, Taylor suggested I sign up for my first ballroom competition at the upcoming Colorado Star Ball. He explained that competing would provide opportunities for practice that my in-studio lessons could not. For example, because dance is a performance art, I would get practice in developing stage presence and overcoming stage fright. Performing in front of others would give me practice in dancing "bigger," meaning with more confident, precise, controlled, energetic movements, the ballroom dancing equivalent of "gettin' down."

Dancing bigger is akin to the Hawthorne Effect, a term referring to the tendency of some people to work harder and perform better when they are being watched, as in a research experiment. Research volunteers often change their behavior simply due to the attention they are receiving. Dancers do, too, I was told.

I also would dance with other couples on the floor, learning how not to play Ballroom Bumper Cars. Because of all this extra practice, Taylor said students who compete often make the fastest strides in their dancing abilities. He reassured me that he would be my partner and we'd have over five months to prepare. He highly recommended I stretch myself to meet this goal. My first reaction was, "You can't be serious." But then that little eight-year-old tap dancer inside of me, who still lusted after lace and sequins, took charge, and I heard someone who sounded a lot like me chirp, "Sure, let's do it."

So from January to June we practiced and practiced and practiced. We drilled seven dances: the waltz, foxtrot, tango, salsa, rumba, East coast swing and the cha cha cha.

As the event drew near Taylor briefed me on what the judges looked for and how their rating system worked. He told me what to eat and drink on the day of the competition, and how to stretch and stay warm between dances. He even politely suggested where I might go to tan my chalky white skin and become a bronzed dancer.

He also gave me a checklist of what to bring:

- Two dance costumes
- Fishnet hose
- A hair piece, if desired--what we call "spare hair"
- False eyelashes
- Make up

- White eyeliner pencil (This makes your eyes look bigger. I brought this but was pretty sure I'd be wide-eyed enough without it.)
- Smooth dance shoes
- Latin dance shoes
- Pins of every kind
- Moleskin
- Band-aids
- Energy bars

I gathered these and the 37 other things on the list. I do not exaggerate. I have gone camping for a week at Machu Picchu with fewer items than I needed for this competition. I compulsively double-checked the list and put everything in my dance duffle bag. On the day of the event I felt like Miss America with a spray tan going on maneuvers.

I felt like I had just landed on an unknown planet from an outer galaxy.

I arrived at the hotel and moved in the direction of the tables with dance merchandise--a rainbow of gowns, shoes and accessories, all with enough bling to put a Vegas showgirl to shame. I knew I'd return to play dress-up, but right now I was totally focused on the competition itself.

I entered the large room where 12 couples, decked out in their sexiest Latin attire, were already on the floor, dancing the salsa. Tears welled up in my eyes from the beauty and the passion. I felt a bolus of adrenalin shoot through my veins. I wanted to pinch myself. *I was about to dance at the Colorado Star Ball!*

I was glad I'd arrived early because I felt like I had just landed on an unknown planet from an outer galaxy. It had been a long time since I'd placed myself in a situation where I truly had no idea what was going to happen. I'd prepared by attending the pre-competition orientation at my studio and had studied the list of dos and don'ts. Taylor and I had practiced each stage of the competition, but there is a lot to remember and I had only recently learned how not to move my lips while I counted the steps in my head. I was delirious, in blissful and complete mental overload.

I wore a stunning short, turquoise, fringed-from-top-to-hem Latin costume. I had never before dressed so sexily in public and I loved it. Getting ready, however, had been quite stressful. That morning, in front of the hotel bathroom mirror, I applied the first false eyelash with ease. Unfortunately, the second one got clumped together with too much glue and try as I might, I could not un-clump it sufficiently to make it match the other one. I looked like I had a hairy spider crawling out of one eye. I fought back tears, correctly surmising that a wet eyelid would not help my cause.

In desperation I went to the ballroom looking for help. A lovely woman in a hot red outfit, more experienced than me in all things dance, including false eyelashes, came to my rescue. She explained (very nicely) that the correct technique to handle these feathery wisps involved applying a thin layer of glue onto the flat curved lash edge, using a toothpick. The incorrect way was what I had done; squeeze a big glob directly from the tube onto the lashes themselves. (Note to self: read the directions first.) As if by magic she tamed the hairs into submission and soon I was back in business, creating a small breeze with every blink.

As I got closer to the dance floor I noticed that the black-attired gentlemen each had a square of white paper with a three-digit number on it pinned on their backs. It was seven in the morning and this was already the sixth heat. I watched group after group perform. I focused on the women, how they walked onto the floor and formally accepted the invitation to dance from their leaders, how they moved to the music and finally, I studied how they took their bows and walked gracefully off the floor, arm in arm with their partners.

And then my heart sank to the bottom of my gut.

Several of these women were incredibly talented. They strutted their stuff around the floor, with moves that Lady Gaga could appreciate. They had perfect posture, following every lead as if it were choreographed. This was the Newcomer Division, for crying out loud, for people who had never competed before and these women danced like pros. I thought, "Oh, sweet Jesus, I'm supposed to compete with them?"

Winning was not uppermost on my mind, and I felt centered enough to know that the event was more about enjoying the experience and simply striving to dance my best rather than besting anyone else. Nevertheless, I certainly did not want to make a fool of myself, and I gotta tell ya, to my beginner's mind, these women danced like divas on fire. It took four more agonizing heats before I figured out that the women who looked like pros WERE pros. In those couples the *gentlemen* were the students. The numbers on the back told the story. Those numbers starting in the one hundreds meant the leader was the pro and the two hundred numbers meant the follower was the pro. This discovery allowed my heart to return to its proper anatomical position in my chest.

I was assigned to compete in heat number 16, which means over 160 dancers had already performed. At 7:30 in the morning Taylor and I joined the other ten pairs of dancers lined up at the corner of the ballroom floor. Then a male voice boomed overhead, "Welcome onto the floor Heat Number 16, dancing the cha cha cha. Music, please." We promenaded out, and the leaders selected their spots. The four judges, with clipboards in hand, stood on the sidelines around the floor, taking notes and ranking the couples in each category. I competed in heat after heat, following the emcees orders, dancing the salsa, rumba and finally the East Coast swing. I was living a dream. When it was over I floated out of the ballroom, counting the hours until tomorrow when I'd get to compete again.

The next day was the smooth dance competition featuring the foxtrot, waltz and tango. I got up early and re-applied my makeup and a new set of lashes that, thanks to the toothpick trick, slid on without a hitch. I donned long, chandelier-drop earrings and styled my hair in a French twist. The Environmental Protection Agency would be very disappointed in the amount of hairspray I used to keep that twist shellacked up on my head.

Then for the really good part: the dress. A ballroom dress can cost four to five thousand dollars so I went to RhythmicRentals.com and rented a gorgeous mint green and jade sequined long gown for $295. Slipping it on that morning, zipping up the back and looking in the mirror-- I only wish I could bottle that feeling and take a swig twice a day. After two hours of Cinderella-going-to the-ball preparations I went back to the dance floor, again at 7:30 a.m. We beginners start at the crack of dawn and the dancing gets progressively more advanced until one in the morning.

My dress, although breathtaking, was a little too long. The proper length is four inches off the floor so your partner does not step on the bottom and trip both of you. The solution, since I could not shorten the hem of the rented dress, meant pinning it tighter to my torso, thereby raising it up the required distance. Which is to say it was really tight. It took a bag of pins and 20 minutes to make this work. The dress had a built in dance pant that you step into as you put the dress on, making high kicks and swirling skirts socially acceptable. So with the help of my fellow dancers in the ladies room I was secured into this gown for the duration. (For those inquiring minds who want to know, snaps in the dance pants solve the problem of visiting the bathroom.)

I went to the practice room solo and tried to "slow, slow, quick, quick" my way into a decent foxtrot. Although eager to dance, I noticed I was surprisingly more nervous than the day before. The fog had lifted and I became more aware of what I was actually attempting and the dangers within. It reminded me of Ty Murray, a nine-time World Champion rodeo cowboy and a contestant on ABC's "Dancing with the Stars." Moments before he performed live in front of 20 million TV viewers, host Tom Bergeron asked him if he was ready to dance next and Ty quipped, "Dancing is like bull riding. You're never really ready; it's just your turn."

I worried most about the tango. It's a tricky little dance with quick turns of the head and positions I had not yet mastered. And because of that, sometimes I'd lead, not on purpose really, more in nervous anticipation, hoping to stay ahead of the next move. Back leading is always a mistake, but especially in the tango, an aggressive dance invented by macho cowboys in Argentinean bordellos. You'd think I'd know better by now.

The emcee called my next heat number and Taylor and I dutifully lined up with the other couples, much like standing in the on-deck circle in baseball, waiting for the announcer to invite us onto the floor. My dress had some accessories, including these gorgeous rhinestone elastic bangles that I'd slipped on my upper arms. Attached to the bangles were three-foot long mint green chiffon streamers, called "floats," designed to flow gracefully as I danced. The streamers would have been an absolutely divine addition to my ensemble if only I had known how to wear them.

The emcee gave us the cue and with heads high and shoulders back we moved ahead to enter the dance floor. Right before I stepped onto the hardwood with my shiny gold dance shoes I felt a force on my arm pulling me back, and I stopped like a horse that has suddenly been reined up short, forcing the couples behind me to stop as well. With what felt like all eyes in the ballroom on me, I jerked my arm forward to wrest myself from whatever was holding me back. My streamer was stuck on the floor.

My mind could not immediately make sense of this. At first, I thought the dancer behind me had stepped on it. But as I turned around and bent down I could see a metal dressmaker's hook on the end of the fabric. My jerking had firmly embedded the hook in the carpet. The metal monster refused to budge. After what seemed like several lifetimes the pro behind me mercifully released it. Taylor, with a look that said simultaneously, "I can't believe you just did that" and "Don't worry, it's okay, let's dance," marched me out to the floor, with the other six delayed couples trailing behind.

Flushed and humiliated, I was sure this had to be the first-of-its kind wardrobe malfunction in the history of dance competition. I later learned that, correctly worn, the metal hooks attach the streamers to the *back of the dress*, creating a wing-like effect. I was a kite when I was supposed to be a butterfly. Well, now I know.

Blessedly, dancing takes you out of your head and into your body. The music starts and transports you to another plane of existence. You dance with your heart, over your foot, and from your powerful core. You ask your critical, judgemental mind to go on safari and leave you alone for a while. In the magic of the next few moments I forgot all about my embarrassment and I just danced.

I must have driven home that night because when I got up the next morning I saw my car parked in the garage. I felt like Gene Kelly and Mario Lopez had danced me back the whole way.

I wish I could tell you what this whole event meant to me

but there are no words. As world-renowned choreographer, Isadora Duncan, said, "If I could tell you what it meant there would be no point in dancing it." All I can offer in way of explanation is this: when someone tells me to go to my happy place, I know right where that is.

My months of practice and overcoming repeated failures did not yet lead to mastery, but I'd inched closer. I competed in 17 heats, winning first or second in 11 of them. I even took first in the tango, which remains a private little joke between Taylor and me because more than once during our dance he urgently and tersely whispered in my ear, "Let me lead!" Nevertheless, I could subtract many hours from the requisite number that I'd need to become a master of this art form. My learning curve still looked like a straight vertical, but, as usual, my instructor was right: the competition itself had been one big eye-opening practice session. I left the competition a much better dancer than I had been two days earlier. And I could not wait to get back to the studio to practice and practice, and practice some more.

Practice

Anyone who has ever taken the next step knows the drill. Practice, fail, practice some more, get better, practice, get worse, wonder if it is all worth it, decide that it is... and so you keep practicing until somehow what you're striving for becomes part of your DNA. Progress usually looks like an erratic, jerky forward movement: two steps forward, one step back.

We do not have to be reminded how difficult this process can be. Our memory usually has fresh examples of the grind.

Even the best in the world acknowledge how hard it is to be good at something. Crusty 'ole Ernest Hemmingway wrote, "There is nothing to writing. All you do is sit down at the typewriter and bleed." Most new endeavors worth doing feel just like that.

It takes commitment to time and often blood, sweat and tears. Christ spent 40 days in the desert working out His problems. He did not say, "Hey, Father, sorry, but I'm really busy. I can maybe give you a long four day weekend, but that's it." No, He showed up at the gym every day to practice His faith.

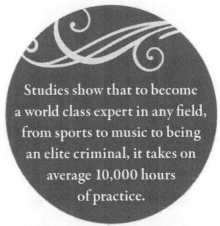

Studies show that to become a world class expert in any field, from sports to music to being an elite criminal, it takes on average 10,000 hours of practice.

Malcolm Gladwell, in his bestselling book, *The Outliers: The Story of Success,* argues that most people who are wildly successful, who've mastered something like Bill Gates and the Beatles did, for example, are not necessarily more talented than everyone else. The real difference lies in their preparation.

Studies show that to become a world class expert in any field, from sports to music to being an elite criminal, it takes on average 10,000 hours of practice.

Before masters gets through the 10,000 hours most hit what author Seth Godin calls "The Dip." He wrote, "The Dip is the long slog between starting and mastery. A long slog that's actually a short cut because it gets you to where you want to go faster than any other path." He described the Dip as "the difference between the easy beginner technique and the more useful expert approach ...the long stretch between beginner's luck and real accomplishment."

We may not be shooting for world mastery, so taking our next step probably won't require 10,000 hours, but research confirms what everyone who has ever learned to ride a bike knows: The more time we put into something, the better we will be. It is important to acknowledge this and get committed.

I like the concept of the Dip because it is easy to see how moving forward can feel like swimming in wet cement. Not only is the experience itself difficult, there is no guarantee that we will ever get out and we fear the possibility we could be forever entombed in concrete. My friend, Susan, in the midst of taking a new direction in her life called me one day and said, "I'm so frustrated! I've called you in lieu of breaking plates. Please remind me again. How long does the Dip last?"

I laughed and told her, "Humans give birth after nine months of incubation. Delivery usually takes less than a day. But being impregnated with ideas and then hatching them can take years, decades, even a lifetime. I suggest you set realistic time tables."

Each person I interviewed for this book admitted to having this experience. Chad Hymas, eager to be self-reliant, discovered in the Dip that it initially took him 90 minutes every morning to put his shirt on. Can you imagine that? After months of practice he now completes the task in six minutes flat. Everyone reported a similar reliance on practice and perseverance. Blessedly, they reaped the rewards for their dedication.

Still, I pressed them. How could they be so disciplined? They each gave the same answer as if it were a self-evident truth: The Dip exists. And a lot of times it is hard. Really, really hard. But if it's worth doing, you push through, ignoring the little voice that says, "Give up." You want it that bad. So day after day you make the effort.

Often our "practice makes perfect" efforts toward a goal seem insurmountable until we break them down into bit-by-bit steps. This reminds me of author Anne Lamott's famous story about her ten-year-old brother, who for three months had procrastinated writing  a school report on birds. It was now due the next day. He sat at the kitchen table, close to tears, surrounded by paper and stacks of unopened books about birds. His father sat down beside him, put his arm around him, and said, "Bird by bird, buddy. Just take it bird by bird."

I love that story because that's exactly what practice is: repetition-by-repetition, do-over-by-do-over, each skill broken down into its smallest part. People who take the next step hold tight to the belief that their bird-by-bird efforts will pay off.

I also love Rita Mae Brown's prayer, "Lead me not into temptation. I can find the way myself." When we set an intention we can guarantee that we will face the temptation to give less than our all, or to put it off until tomorrow or next week or when we have more money, time or motivation. We will have days when giving up entirely seems like the only reasonable option, like throwing out a gallon jug full of sour milk. We're convinced the situation could not possibly improve. Yielding to these temptations does not make us bad; it makes us human. Remember that and be very gentle with yourself when the inevitable see-saw of progress makes you doubt. Because you can do this.

So why does practice work? It works because when we practice we create pathways--neurological, musculoskeletal, creative, spiritual pathways--through which energy can flow. The operative concept here is energy flow.

Case in Point: The Healing Power of Practice

Douglas Victor Eagle was a 20-year-old Junior World Racquetball Champion who could hit the ball 180 miles an hour *and* return one going that same speed just as well.

"Acceptance made it easy to see what relieved the pain. Once I saw the trail, I was just running it."

He was soaring to a bright career as a top pro player when a reckless driver ran a red light, crushing his small sports car, sending it spinning wildly. Following the accident he was in agony from both the intractable pain of a serious lower back injury and the news from his doctors who gave Eagle no hope of returning to his beloved sport and fulfilling his dream of becoming a top-ranking professional athlete. His disappointment, fear and physical pain were overwhelming. "I was bitter," he confessed. "I asked, 'Is there a God? The other driver was unscathed. How is that fair?' I was angry and full of self-pity."

Through several months of unimaginable pain and despair, he made a commitment to rebuild his life. "First," he said, "I had to accept where I was with the pain. Any movement at all caused it. Accepting my pain was the start because then I knew how to get out. I knew I could not skip this step because if I did I would just keep going back to it. Acceptance made it easy to see what relieved the pain. Once I saw the trail, I was just running it."

Two years after the car crash, in the best physical and mental condition of his life, Eagle defied the naysayers and returned to the tour, subsequently winning back-to-back Texas State Singles titles and making the national team twice. He played professionally for seven more years, ranked as one of the top ten best players in the world.

How did he do this? "Practice," he said. "I practiced Ashtanga yoga for hours a day, day after day, for two years. I kept getting better, and that nurtured me along. I found I could heal every day at whatever level I chose by getting out of my head and just having an awareness of my breath."

"Pain was my teacher," he continued. "The breath is the monitor of the pain. I had to listen to the feeling in my heart and not the logic in my mind."

I asked him how two years of yoga practice affected his athletic skill level.

He said, "When I returned to the pro ranks I was an infinitely better player because of my yoga practice. My improvement was much more than just physical. I was so present in stressful situations on the court. My play was beyond thought. I knew if I could see the racket strings touch the ball as I hit it, if I could see the point of contact in my mind, I had already won the match."

He was so "tripped out" by yoga he took yet another step.

"I was at the top of my game when I decided to retire from professional sports and devote myself to the practice of yoga. I wanted to be a pioneer, teaching fellow athletes a new way to be their best," he explained.

He sold all his real estate and business ventures, liquidating nearly everything he owned. Then he spent months each year studying with Sri K. Pattabhi Jois in Mysore, India.

"I am deeply inspired by my teacher, one of the world's preeminent yoga masters, who represents teaching lineages extending back for thousands of years. He was the real deal. I saw his energy, presence and vitality. His devotion to yoga spanned more than seven decades. I live by his advice: 'Theory 1%. Practice 99%.'"

Eagle has now dedicated himself to teaching others the techniques that elevated him out of pain and into physical and emotional bliss.

The breathing technique that Eagle performs with his practice is called ujjayi pranayama, which means "victorious breath."

How fitting.

It's Simple

I was blessed to study under Eagle for two months while I lived in Kauai. I'm telling you, he's something else. He can wrap his legs around his neck three times and then grab his toes--with a smile on his face. He personifies discipline. He gets up at four in the morning six days a week to spend two hours doing his practice and then sits in meditation for 20 minutes several times a day. He is an attentive, compassionate, enlightened yoga teacher for his devotees from 7:30 am to 9:30 am on those same six days. He is a strict organic vegan and he looks absolutely radiant and ageless. He strives to live a life in which awareness is his only purpose. Period. I suspect when he chants the birds stop singing so they can listen. Did I mention he can wrap his legs around his neck three times? Got all that? Good. It should make the little bit of practice we are resisting melt away in comparison.

Eagle's philosophy of life continues to inspire me. I have summarized his teachings into four words that I strive to live by: *Practice simply. Simply practice.*

Accepting the Invitation

Dear Mary,

I have been thinking about this idea of "practice" and how it applies to moving forward in life. First, I must tell you that I am a recovering perfectionist. I don't know when the idea of perfectionism got a hold of me, but somewhere I decided if I couldn't do it and do it well, then I wasn't going to even try. As I write that, it makes me wonder how many things I was inspired by along the way that I didn't even give a try, because I would have to practice to get good at: The piano lessons I gave up on when I was in elementary school because I didn't like to practice; the golf games with my dad that I walked away from because I couldn't play well enough; the relationships that frustrated me when they didn't meet my expectations and instead of leaning in and discovering new skills, I let them fade away; the writing I didn't do because I would need to write and rewrite to get good at it; and the disappointment I have felt with my spirituality when I didn't attain enlightenment with a few sittings of meditation.

Oh my, the list could go on.

But wait, I am in my late forties and I must say I am inspired by this idea of practice. I now notice the perfectionism that has driven me to achieve and not feel like anything is good enough is fading in my rearview mirror. I find myself delighting in reading and exploring new avenues of thought, not because I need to fix something in myself or others, but because "I like to practice." I like to practice at this thing called life and see in what ways I can grow and master new levels of learning and living. How do you do this, but to practice?

As a kid I loved basketball. My mother had played basketball in Oklahoma when the women played 3 on 3. We didn't have basketball for girls in Nebraska, but she and my father told me if I learned to play I would have my opportunity. I'd practice late into the evening underneath the streetlight learning to dribble with both hands and not look at the ball. I went through the fundamentals again and again with the delight and joy of simple improvements. I played for hours by myself for the simple love of the game.

Oddly enough, I loved to practice basketball. And isn't it fascinating to think that we spend way more time in practice than we do an actual game? My town did get basketball for girls when I was a freshman in high school. I would go on to become one of the first Division I female college athletes on a *full ride scholarship. For me, the practices were always the place I allowed myself to learn and grow and course correct some of the mistakes that may have appeared in my game.*

What if it is that way in life?

What if we are here to practice? To practice at being better in the relationships that matter to us? To practice being more committed to our well-being emotionally, mentally, spiritually and physically? To practice listening to our Source and applying what we learn? To practice being better today at going gently with ourselves as well as others? To practice radical self-care? To practice leaning into our fears gingerly with small steps and let go of the pressure to have it all figured out?

I thank you for the example you have demonstrated through your passion and commitment to dance. You love your lessons and the two hours of practice. Of course you feel frustrated that you have not mastered dancing but that doesn't keep you from dancing practice after practice.

So today I lay down this notion and expectation that my relationships, my career, my finances, and my health must be perfect and tidy and wrapped in a bow. I untie the bow and lift the lid off, allowing for breathing space in the delightful exploration of all there is to be discovered. And in each of these areas I will take what matters to me and repeat it again and again and again. Why? Because each of them matter to me and I am willing to practice.

And how grateful I am for every moment I get to begin again.

Thank you for your inspiration,
--Melanie Mills

THE LESSON: *PRACTICE*

Again.
Again.
Again.
*And again.**

Take Your Next Step

What do you need to practice?

*And again.

Chapter Ten

───────o◦⟨⟩◦o───────

The Grand Finale

───────o◦⟨⟩◦o───────

And the time came when the risk to remain tight in a bud was more painful than the risk it took to blossom.

--Anais Nin

About 18 months after I first began my dance lessons I was invited to speak to an association of credit advisors in New York City. I was scheduled to give the closing keynote on my specialty, life balance strategies. In addition, during the hour before that program, I was booked to present a breakout session. On a whim I decided it would be called, "What If the Hokey Pokey Really Is What It's All About." And--in a moment when the frontal cortex of my brain, without the benefit of alcohol or drugs, somehow became completely disinhibited--I decided to fly Manny out to the city that never sleeps to dance a little number for the finale with me.

I know. I know what you're wondering, "New York City? Credit advisors? Dance? What could she have possibly been thinking?"

Clearly, I wasn't.

Nevertheless, Manny and I practiced for weeks. I felt confident I knew the choreography and even felt comfortable with my ever-improving beginner's ability. Our performance looked surprisingly good on videotape. How exciting, I mused. My dream is coming true. I am actually going to perform a dance on stage in the Big Apple!

The travel day arrived and we flew from Denver to New York. Manny and I met for a dress rehearsal in the morning the day before the event. To say that my dancing was horrible would be an understatement at its zenith. I was nervous and tensed up. I fought the turns and could not stay on the beat. I got flustered and couldn't remember the salsa routine to save my soul. The more we practiced the worse I got. My confidence eroded and I wondered to myself, "How can I get out of this? There is no way I can perform in front of 125 conference attendees, the meeting planner, and the sponsor of my event and look like this clumsy moron. Calgon, take me away!"

While Manny remained incredibly patient and supportive I was beating myself up and frantically doing my best to stave off panic. I thought, "Great. First, I will make a fool of myself in the breakout session. Then I'll have to go next door to the large ballroom and speak to 400 people after I've completely humiliated myself."

My mind searched for escape routes. I prayed again, "Good Lord, how do I get out of this? Get lost in the subway? Feign a heart attack? Have a nervous breakdown?" I might not have to fake the latter.

After two hours of grueling practice I did one run-through correctly. Not brilliantly, but good enough. Manny said, "Okay. That's it. We're done now."

"No", I pleaded. "Let's practice some more."

Manny got firm. "Mary! Listen to me. You know how to dance this routine. Trust me. Trust yourself. You'll be great tomorrow. Let's take our tickets and go to the Broadway shows now and just relax."

So I reluctantly obeyed my coach and we attended two fabulous shows, a matinee and an evening performance. There's nothing like watching people dance on Broadway to make you really feel like a five-legged centipede. I wanted to throw up.

When I got back to the hotel I tried to sleep, but I spent most of the night mentally going over the dance routine. It wasn't just the fear of a bruised ego that was keeping me awake. I deeply respect my audiences and take my responsibility to deliver a high quality program very seriously. It's challenging enough to customize a speech for my clients, and yet now I'd decided to add another layer of complexity. I lay in bed wondering, "Am I just having stage fright or did I really make a huge mistake by deciding to dance? Am I bringing my passion to work or having a midlife crisis? Is this my career unfolding or have I gone totally insane?"

Is this my career unfolding or have I gone totally insane?

When I did doze off I dreamed I had committed professional suicide in high heels and fishnet hose. This scenario is not as far-fetched as you might think. Meeting planners take my responsibility to delight the audience as seriously as I do, and they understandably set the bar quite high. Details of a botched performance in the meetings industry spread like Hollywood gossip and can quickly derail an otherwise stellar career. The next morning I woke up with a ball of anxiety in the pit in my stomach the size of Detroit.

Manny and I only had time for a quick and entirely inadequate 15-minute dance warm-up before my breakout session began. I told the audience about the life balance lessons I had learned from my ballroom dance experience. The program went great, the attendees were insightful and engaged, and I loved feeling so connected to them.

But in the back of my mind I was making getaway plans.

Five minutes before the end of my presentation I took a deep breath, looked out at the audience, and said, "For the last 55 minutes I have been *telling* you what dance has taught me about life. I would now like to *show* you what that looks like."

With that I turned around, walked upstage (away from the audience) and with my back to them, I struck a diva pose. Manny rose from his front row seat, and took off his black jacket, revealing a black sequined vest and tie. Smiling like he had just realized what Victoria's secret really is, he flamboyantly donned a matching black sequined fedora. I heard the audience take a collective gasp. While Manny captured their attention I slipped my lapel microphone in my pocket and unbuttoned my black business jacket. From stage right Manny did a triple turn over to me and dramatically slipped my jacket off my shoulders and threw it off stage. He turned on the music with a tiny remote and the staccato salsa music filled the room. As we spun around in unison to face the audience, I heard another gasp as the attendees saw *my* costume: a black, sequined halter-top and black dance pants. I felt hooked up to an IV drip of joy juice as I attempted to channel *West Side Story*'s Chita Rivera with every muscle fiber I had.

Surrendering to Manny's competent lead, I got out of my head and relaxed into the salsa beat. My body took over and performed the best it ever has. I'm not sure if I relaxed because I was so totally in the moment or if I was simply hypoxic. I'll probably never know but I will tell you my racing heart was happy, happy, happy.

The last move of our performance was a dramatic backward dip into Manny's arms. On the way back up I grabbed the fedora off his head and wore it to take my bow. I looked out at the crowd, who by then were on their feet clapping and sporting grins as big as mine. I am not sure which of us was more surprised at what had just happened.

I motioned for them to sit back down, moved closer to the front of the stage and addressed them once more:

"In ballroom dance competition, there are three main levels: bronze, silver and gold. I am considered 'pre-bronze'. Translated this means if I was playing soccer I would be second string in the peewee league.

"So here we are in New York City, where there are literally hundreds of thousands of people standing around on street corners who can dance better than I can. And worldwide, there are millions, if not billions who can dance more competently than I could ever dream of. So why on earth would I get up in front of an audience and dance as a novice?

"Well...professional speakers will do just about anything to make a point. And here it is:

Although there are billions who can dance *better* than I can, I believe there are no dancers anywhere who have felt *more passionately and blissfully alive* than I just did in the last two minutes and thirty eight seconds.

"And THAT, ladies and gentlemen, is what the Hokey Pokey is *really* all about."

With that I invited them to stand and together we did a rafter-shaking rendition of the famous verse:

You put your right foot in.
You put your right foot out.
You put your right foot in and you shake it all about.
You do the Hokey Pokey and you turn yourself around.
That's what it's all about.

And the curtain closed.

So what about you? Maybe you've lost your house, your confidence, or what feels like your mind. Maybe you know you should get out of the dead end job and go back to school. Perhaps you've (as the Brits say when you get laid off) "been made redundant," and you are not quite sure what to do next. Or it could be that you need to get out of your marriage, your town or your own way. You wouldn't have read this far if you didn't have an intense desire to take your next step. I hope this book holds some truths for you. You may have discovered other lessons as you read. Write to me and tell me about them. I am a student of life just like you are.

The ideas presented here do not describe a lock-step process. Everyone I talked to said they made additional requests and continued to refine their intentions. They found new things to quit, surrendered to more leads, and circled back around to ambiguity, which required more disinhibition. They kept doing their basics over and over. Practice and failure were constants, and partners often popped up in places they least expected.

My goal in writing this book is to help you organize your thinking as you take your next step. I have no pat answers, but I do have a passionate desire to help you ask the right questions. I believe the first step begins with keeping your senses attuned to that still small voice that knows. Everything. All the time. The word on the street is that every first step begins and ends with awareness.

I hope that the stories of the extraordinary people you've read about in these pages have inspired you to move forward. As I reflect back on their journeys I can see they had many things in common. Like Renee Bates, who could not quit the LSAT test, they all made honest self-assessments of their strengths and weaknesses. They also all reported being optimists. None of them knew *how* but they believed in the inevitability that things would work themselves out. They did what the most successful CEOs did in Jim Collins book, *Good to Great*. They faced the (often brutal) truth, and still kept an optimistic attitude that their problems would be overcome. They all said the words that Chad's wife, Shondell uttered, "Well, I didn't really have a choice." Of course they had a choice. Actually they had a cornucopia of choices including staying stuck, wallowing around in self-pity or running away to the circus with the Amazing Pretzel Man. My best friend, Brenda, calls their kind of perseverance, "having the ability to stay in the room." They accepted the "is-ness" of their realities, and once they made their choices, they acted. They did not wait for Glinda the Good Witch to touch them with her wand. They believed they could make their own magic, step-against-all-odds-step.

They also used forgiveness to take them to a higher level of consciousness. Eagle forgave the driver who hit him saying, "She was a blessing in disguise, prompting me to really look at my life. She propelled me into an evolution I might not have had without the extreme pain." Nicolette, Scott and a few others said they forgave and dismissed their "old God" and crafted a new, more enlightened version, one that was personal to them and not based on the dogma they were raised with.

None of them think they have arrived nor are they without problems. Melanie continues to view life as way to "practice simply and simply practice." Nick doesn't know just what he's going to be when he grows up. He is currently traveling the Silk Road in Asia, much like Marco Polo did, only with lots of Apple accessories. Ann, a beautiful woman with a lithe body that belies her seventy-two years, speaks for all of them when she says she's happier now than ever before. They are all grateful for their journeys and report finding a peace they did not know to the depths they do now, even though life is not perfect.

There was one unintended outcome of facing their challenges. The experience of stepping out greatly expanded their capacity for compassion, which they pass on to others. They found a way to give back, to ease the pain or show the way for the next person on a similar path. Chad works with other quadriplegics, being their inspiring Art Berg. Nick volunteered at an orphanage in Ghana for AIDS orphans. My wise friend, Kris, who I quote so often, films artful videos of terminally ill children as a priceless gift for their families. Joan served as the spokesperson for Prevent Blindness America. Maryam tutored a fellow Iranian beauty school student who spoke no English, helping her graduate and get a self-supporting job. I could mention each one of them and illustrate how they have made their life a shining example of a deepened compassion.

They have also encouraged others to give, enlarging their circle of influence. Melanie, Brenda, Donna, and Manisha work tirelessly to empower women. At the Texas Roadhouse convention each year Kent and the company's 1100 managing partners and spouses spend one full day doing community service in the host city. During their annual conference in San Francisco, for example, the TRH donated one million dollars in labor and materials for Habitat for Humanity. Sangay is a newspaper columnist/activist, writing passionately about how to keep in place the Kingdom of Bhutan's designation as one of the happiest places on earth. Karyn is the president of the Association of Applied and Therapeutic Humor, encouraging others to live amazed and amused. Linda teaches coroners about the syndrome of sudden death from epilepsy; Jane wrote a book on love called *The Frog*

Whisperer; and Eagle, who continues to teach Ashtanga yoga on the island of Kauai, is raising money to build a temple.

I mention this compassion concept in detail because one of the tenets of my life's work is that it is impossible for connection to go one way. They proved me right. They are all bridge builders in their own unique ways. They could have each authored the following poem:

> *The Bridge Builder*
> *An old man going a lone highway*
> *Came at the evening, cold and gray,*
> *To a chasm vast and wide and steep,*
> *With waters roiling cold and deep.*
> *The old man crossed in the twilight dim,*
> *The sullen stream had no fears for him;*
> *But he turned when safe on the other side,*
> *And built a bridge to span the tide.*
> *"Old man," said a fellow pilgrim near,*
> *"You are wasting your strength with building here.*
> *Your journey will end with the ending day,*
> *You never again will pass this way.*
> *You've crossed the chasm deep and wide,*
> *Why build you this bridge at eventide?"*
>
> *The builder lifted his old gray head.*
> *"Good friend, in the path I have come," he said,*
> *"There followth after me today*
> *A youth whose feet must pass this way.*
> *The chasm that was as nought to me*
> *To that fair-haired youth may a pitfall be.*
> *He, too, must cross in the twilight dim.*
> *Good friend, I am building this bridge for him.*

Will Allen Dromgoole (d. 1934)

Where Are You Now?

I hope that you found the exercises at the end of the chapters instructional. I think it is helpful to view yourself as a "fair-haired youth" and examine the possible pitfalls. One woman did just that and wrote to me:

Dear Mary,

I spent some time assessing how I was using the strategies you propose for moving forward. You have made it easy to see where I am falling short.

First of all, I'm not surrendering. I've never even considered it a good idea, much less something I would strive to do. I regularly beat myself to a pulp over every last little "failure," and I most definitely have some things I need to quit (like harboring anger over my former business partner). And while I've kept up my financial basics I have not kept up my health basics. I've become one of those 83 percent of people trying to lose weight by lowering their caloric intake while saying, "I don't have time" to exercise. As for meditating--don't get me started. My dad has been telling me for years I don't have the time not to meditate. And until I address these issues, truly, I'm not going to be able to take that vital next step forward. In fact, I can see that I may have to first step back and even patiently step in place. But what I've done is jump smack into practice without doing any of the other bits. As I'm painfully learning, sheer force of will can only take you so far when your change foundation is shaky.

Ready, Set, Step

So here are the CliffsNotes: Ask for what you really want. Set your intention for the highest good and let the quarks have a play date. Quit all the things that are in the way. Agree to live comfortably for a time in IhavenoideawhatIamdoingville. Take Sully's advice: what you fear is not going to be as bad  as you think. Dance the international rumba every once in a while and be sure to put a little wiggle in it. For God's sake surrender the lead and get into the flow of life. Keep doing your basic steps, find harmonious partners to help you, and then practice, fail, practice, fail, practice some more and strive for mastery. Believe in the power of the human spirit.

One evening as I left a hotel restaurant in Princeville, Hawaii, I stopped at the bell stand to inquire if the one-mile hike back to my rented condo would be safe for me to walk alone at night. The twenty-something handsome Hawaiian bellman said, "Oh, sure, it's very safe, except that the sidewalk will be quite dark and you might trip. Wait here a minute, please." With that he ran off into the adjacent parking lot to his car, and when he returned he handed me a flashlight the size and shape of a large ice cube. It had an elastic band that slipped over your wrist like a bracelet.

"Here," he offered, "so you can see the path better in the darkness. Oh, and my name is Paul. Just send the light back to me before you leave the island."

The feeling I had at that moment is exactly how I want you to feel about this book. It is my small gift of light to you. I invite you to use it to illuminate your path, to brighten your way in the darkness. Oh, and my name is Mary. Just send the light back to me before you leave the planet.

Accepting the Invitation

Dear Readers,

So there you have it: A 223-page formal written invitation to take your next step. I hope that you received the lessons that will guide you, the inspiration that will lift you and a clear vision of just how good moving forward can feel. I especially hope that each morning you accept the invitation with joy.

I stand by as your virtual partner, looking forward to hearing about your experiences, the "dance steps" that you find most helpful, your ahas and your successes. I just hope I can sleep what with all the noise from the quarks that will be collapsing in perfect synchronicity around the globe. Please stay connected at MaryLoVerde@gmail.com.

Warmest aloha,

Mary

About the Author

*M*ary LoVerde is an internationally-acclaimed life balance expert and the author of three best-selling books: *I Used to Have a Handle on Life but It Broke; Stop Screaming at the Microwave;* and *Touching Tomorrow.*

Mary has shared her innovative, step-by-step strategies for a balanced life with audiences from Bangkok to Biloxi, to clients as diverse as the Mayo Clinic, AT&T and the American Trucking Association. She has appeared on 20/20, ABC World News Tonight, and four times on the Oprah Winfrey show. She is a former faculty member of the University of Colorado School of Medicine and for 15 years served as the director of the Hypertension Research center. Her original work has appeared in the three "most important" journals: The New England Journal of Medicine, The Wall Street Journal and The Ladies Home Journal.

In 2009 Speaker Magazine named Mary as one of the 25 most influential speakers shaping the industry. In 2010 the National Speakers Association inducted her into the Speaker's Hall of Fame.

Also in 2009 Mary accepted an unexpected invitation to sell her one-of-a-kind dream home, give away nearly all her belongings, and embark on a make-it-up-as-you-go global adventure. Her motto is "At home wherever I am."

The people she met and the lessons she learned have become the genesis of the "I-Accept-the-Invitation" Movement. Visit maryloverde.com to see fun, fascinating videos of people from around the world who have said yes...and share your own.

You can reach Mary at MaryLoVerde@gmail.com or www.maryloverde.com.

Have You Read Mary's Other Books?

What a wonderful collection of simple, practical ways to reconnect deeply with people that matter in your life. I highly recommend this book.
--Jack Canfield
Chicken Soup for the Soul

I used your book, Touching Tomorrow to interview my 76-year-old father. Giving him an opportunity to "say his piece" gave him "peace" Everyone should create a priceless gift like this before it is too late.
--Sean O'Brien

Mary, thanks for your book 'Mulheres que fazem demais'. Did you come into my house with a video camera? How do you know exactly how we Braziian women think?
-- Eliane, Brazil

Thanks to My Professional Dance Partners
Taylor Westfall

*T*aylor Westfall began dancing at age 15. He quickly made a name for himself as a professional dancer. He travels the US competing in the Professional American Rhythm division with his dance partner, Jennifer Corey. Together they have won both the 2010 Colorado and the 2010 Seattle Rising Star and Open Rhythm championships and the 2008 Golden State Rising Star Rhythm competition. They are also the 2008 International Grand Ball Rising Star Rhythm Champions.

Taylor is renowned for his teaching abilities and is a much sought after coach. He has won numerous national Top Teacher awards and in 2009 placed eighth in the Global Top Teacher awards. His attention to technique and details in performance has helped his students consistently place high in competition. He is now an instructor and coach at Booth's Dancesport in Denver, Colorado.

I want to thank him for allowing me to be his student. The second he hits the dance floor his enthusiasm for the art of dancing is simply contagious. He has brought such joy into my life, teaching me about the beauty of movement, and how to use my body to express the music and my emotions. In a perfect world I'd have a lesson with him every day.

Manny Viarrial

*M*anny Viarrial has been dancing for 32 years. In high school and college his specialty was "street hustle" and he won dance contests all over town. He then fell in love with the west coast swing and studied with some of the best. His dedication paid off. He is now a former West Coast Swing US Open Dance champion and in 2011 the Rocky Mountain Swing Club inducted him into the Hall of Fame.

This gifted dancer and instructor has earned more than 150 first place titles over the course of his amazing career, and has won dozens of Top Teacher awards at competitions nationwide. His greatest joy, however, comes from helping others learn how to dance and watching them become graceful, skilled, accomplished dancers. His devoted students regularly place in the top three.

You can see him dance on youtube at www.DanceManny.com.

I am blessed to study with him. He teaches from 9-9 and at the end of this long day, when the last students arrive in his studio he greets them with an attitude that says, "Oh, I am so glad you are here! I have been looking forward all day to dancing with you." Manny believes the Indian proverb, "To watch us dance is to hear our hearts speak." He introduced me to the beauty and the bliss of dancing and I am eternally grateful.